MONSTERS INSIDE

ME

I0704074

MONSTERS INSIDE ME

Understand the secret of your thoughts and how life responds to you...

Claire Awada, PhD

(Specialized in Metaphysical Psychology)

Copyright © 2015 Claire Awada
All Rights Reserved.

All rights reserved by author. No part of this publication may be reproduced, stored in a retrieval system or transmitted in any form or by any means, electronic, mechanical, photocopy recording or otherwise, without the prior permission of the author. Published by author.

The views expressed in this book are entirely those of the author. The printer/ publisher, and distributors of this book are not in any way responsible for the views expressed by the author in this book. All disputes are subject to arbitration; legal actions if any are subject to the jurisdictions of court of Kolkata, India.

ISBN-13: 978-1983594786

First Published: 2015

Price: $16.99

Cover Design

Rajarshi Ghosh

Distributed by flipkart.com
power-publishers.com
purushottam-bookstore.com ebay.in

Acknowledgement

In dedication to my father

To everyone one who inspired me

To those has no one to help them

Those whose hearts ache, through ego and limiting belief

To everyone wants to fly towards their dreams.

Contents

Introduction

Life is- a gift placed in our hands as we make our way into this world. As any other gift we receive, it depends on us as to how best it is utilized or just whiled away through mere existence. Why is it that we ourselves are witness to lives being lived in front of us in all its majestic form and meanwhile some lives just being pushed around, trying to still find its right meaning? This question kept knocking into horizons of my mind, beyond my comfort level, pushing me to find means which channelize any human existence to find their way to maximum potential possible. Sometimes it may be a varied number of circumstances or situations which pushes us to question our relevance in the world. The world we live in is changing at a pace beyond anyone's grasp most of the times! Each one of us is trying their level best to keep up in best method possible, few stay afloat and for some the process becomes very challenging.

Living a life which may give you a vitalizing thrill from within is where we all want to be. Accomplishing anything great all the time may not be our individual intention, yet to derive satisfaction in your career, relationships, finances and other facets of our life becomes the bench mark. There has to be a success formula which we could all follow, but, there exists none as each life has a different story. Its only when I embarked on a journey beyond the comfort zone of living my life as a professional and a mother of two, did it strike me that somewhere I needed to make a difference in lives as I keep making in my own, and those that are connected to me in different spheres. Drawing examples from my own life and those around me, it became slowly yet painfully evident that the power to live the way you want and the changes you want to bring about, has always been in our hands. It's just that we were not aware and it consciously doesn't dawn into our minds, till it is pointed out by another person in the right perspective.

The awareness that as individuals in this Earth, we are not merely here to exist as independent units but to make a difference in others' lives too, to reduce the pain and hardships many faces in life. Being in the know that we need to change some facets of our lives is the beginning. Change has often been understood as a process which by definition is difficult in our minds, we find difficult to inculcate it, and find comfortably numb in practicing what has been happening always, but it remains to be understood that change sometimes is also for the best!!! To bring about anything different than what is presently happening, needs pushing our own selves beyond our comfort zones. To move from mediocre to inspiring is journey which is difficult yet achievable by each one of us. At this juncture it does not matter where you are but it definitely matters where you want to reach. It is then that the conviction in your own self needs to rise beyond what you have believed till now.

As these words of the book reach you, you will realize there is unlimited power within you, waiting to be unleashed, and may wane away if never touched upon in the right way. At this stage the biggest mistake you could do is to believe that it is beyond your reach and succumb to the feeling of fear within you which tends to overpower each of us when we tend to start a journey within. Just beat it down with your faith and go beyond. I learnt to hold my thoughts together as they formed the basis of what I would believe, and I decided that I could and I did. If I could, so can you as there lay vast potential around to scale any cliff.

Let us emerge above the daily grind and let me take you on a journey long postponed to spread the message of kindness, faith in humanity beyond me and mine, show hope to selves and others to accomplish what we always only dreamt of in our lives. If you wait forever for things to happen to you, for confirming every single step you take is right then maybe you may never get to doing anything at all. There are some risks of faith you have to dig in and follow your intuition with a well-intended intention and you will be there. Make the choices; take the chances and the right changes will occur as time goes. Just because the past didn't turn out like you wanted it to, absolutely does not imply that your future cannot be better than you ever imagined. Take things in your hand and the will to follow it and success is bound to happen.

Sometimes you have to just believe that a decision you make can change the entire course of your life, the change can come to you in strangest of places or from most unexpected of people yet be ready to see beyond the scene. It may be a single thing and you may just be flooded with series of changes that happen as you go. Be willing to go with the flow when it does come to you. Have the conviction that what you decide today will transform your destiny. Coincidences are only a way of making it easier in your life. As I stand today, I am licensed NLP coaching trainer™, a wonderful set of teaching and techniques transforming lives with the power invested in our own selves, I take the view that you will find your calling and happiness if you so desire so .The universe stands to aid you in this journey. Take the plunge, take the responsibility for it and you shall find yourself at peace beyond you can ever imagine. I am grateful to my family and friends for standing by me in all my endeavors and supporting in all their capacity.

CHAPTER 1: I AM

Who Are We? What Is The Meaning Of 'I' In Us?

All of us at some point of our lives have questioned our worth. There may have been failures, rebukes may have come our way or at times bouts of depression may have resulted in us questioning our worth. The existence of the cosmic structure and the reason for one's existence has been a highly debated topic with no clear winners. Each one of us have experienced the effect other human beings in our immediate proximity have had in shaping our lives. The development of our brain as we grow up in life and age is something which is intriguing to everyone who has given it some thought! The brain matures every day getting enriched with facts, knowledge, multiple thought processes and ways to understand life as it comes. This is always existent and happens till the second we depart from this world!

Well, now virtual identity takes care of one beyond the real world of people. Even the identity we hold as a person has always had two sides to it, like that of a coin!! One side being the unique self as an individual, and the other self in relation to others in the society or the social identity. Eventually both lead to meet as one, to have the whole coin.

What is the meaning of "I am"? Who am I? Am I just a name, an identity amongst millions of lives roaming around me on this world every day? Am I a mere number or do I have any unique identity in this world infested by humans? Our past experiences mold us into what we are today, in fact while writing this I am discovering a new identity of myself that I didn't know I have, and future interplay of actions, environment, situation and people around me will shape me to be what I will be. It's a curious interplay of various factors that define who "I am". As I write this book, I realized how the monster 'Teratoma' seated deeply within me has been eating away into my tissues and cells, possessing the ability of growing human cells without ever becoming a human embryo. The most horrifying and alarming information about this tumor Teratoma is that, it has the ability to grow hair and teeth that are very similar to real human tissues. Some teratoma contain mature tissues such as hair follicles, fat tissue, sweat glands, partially or fully developed nerve tissue, and tissues strongly resembling human teeth. Teratoma usually form in the ovaries of women, testes of men and in the sacrum (large triangle shaped bone found at the end of the spinal column) of children. The prognosis of a patient with a teratoma varies highly depending on the case and the location and growth of the tumor. Caught quite awestruck by this information about Teratoma, and me being its carrier, I contemplated- Who am I physiologically, emotionally, spiritually? How frequently would this 'I' in me keep transforming with the changes that happen in these three spheres?

While I was researching to pen down a few thoughts playing hide and seek, I came to interesting conclusions as to what "I am" means. In Indian Mythology the concept of "Om", is the first sound of the universe. Recent researches into discoveries of planets and galaxies also conclude that they have found a sound that actually equates the sound recorded as "Om". Now what is 'Om'? It is supposed to be the healing power and sound of the universe, the way practically our maker connects to us. In meditation and yoga this sound of "Om" is highly used to relax and to get connected to the inner self and to who I am. The "I am" power can be felt as a strong inspiration to some with great wisdom, patience, practice and for gaining knowledge. Remember Buddha getting enlightenment under a tree? It's the same kind of self revelation, understanding and knowledge that one gains after embracing solitude from everyday life and surrendering to greater forces of which we are made of. There is no limit to the power of "I am" when it comes to healing and transforming ones aspect of life.

When our body gets wounded, our cells, tissues and fibers heal all by themselves after some time. Mind however is different, when it gets wounded, it sometimes takes months and sometimes years to forget, forgive and move on. In short, to heal itself from all the negative energy it faced. But never the less it heals for which time is the best medicine it can have. I have the power of healing "I am", capable of curing and getting a better 'myself', maybe by just a Nano millionth of the strength the universe has. But I can, and I am capable of doing that and we do encounter people with such reputations. Starting from Jesus, it is said he could cure people's illness and troubles, with just his magic touch. We see acupressure, we see hypnosis, we see people getting well with Reiki, miracles happen with hermits looking at pictures and healing the person who is in body miles away. These are all fragments of energy being transferred from one to another. Some have greater psychic powers than normal, and use these to transform and heal individuals, get them out of the misery, agony and pain. It's a greater strength acquired by some. As energy flows from one to another, we can best refer to it as an energy flown from the universe or "Om" or developed from inside as a product of "I am". It is power an energy that comes from within, it's neither good nor bad, and it's up to us to make it good or bad. Lord Shiva in Indian mythology is considered to be the greatest hermit of all times. He is said to be sitting on the top of mountain Kailash lost in his own meditation and thoughts. Some say sometimes he would open his eyes, say "tathastu" and go back to meditation again. "Tathastu" (meaning your wish will be granted) is a magic word. Say you are saying to yourself "I am a looser, I can never get admission to that university" and accidentally Lord Shiva says "tathastu" and you are doomed! Imagine yourself saying "I am capable of getting this job, and will give my best in the interview", what about a "tathastu" to that??? It's you, you yourself can enable the positivity's or the negativities in your mind to make or build a halo of energy around you. "I am" the best painter to decide whether it will be good or bad for me. When you say something negative about yourself the powers inside you gets limited. Instead you can insist that "I am" capable and it gives an immense capacity to mold or transform yourself.

Our existence hinges on our identity, just like the door to your house. Were we to imagine our survival without an identity, the idea itself would sound insane!!Can a house exist without doors or the doors without the support of walls of the house…simple, no! I exist; I live because "I am", so it is with you or rather any of us. The self-discovery of a person can be initiated at any stage, age or crossroad of life. How do you become 'you', how does the 'I' of 'I am 'evolve besides having been born as a human.

'I' Am Being A Part Of The Divine:

Often God is known as "I am". Do you hear the little voices in your head that tells you what to do? Call it the call of your heart or mind games; it actually inspires you to take all the decisions in your life. For a normal person it is impossible to stay in a blank state of mind, constantly one thought or the other crops up, tell you memories, experiences, probabilities and makes you do things.

The "I am" power is inundated with Judeo- Christian as well as Eastern religious beliefs. Jesus said *"I am the light of the world"*.

The Sufi poet Rumi has been found to say;
"I am neither a Muslim nor a Hindu;
I am not a Christian, Zoroastrian, nor a Jew;
My place is the no place
My image is without face
Neither of body nor the soul
I am of the divine whole"

Truly we are all part of the divine, the cosmic powers of the universe and have been gifted a little of that in every one. It's up to us how do we perceive "I am" to be. For it's through our eyes that the rest of the world will see it. It doesn't matter who thinks what about us. It's how we perceive ourselves in our own eyes that matters the most. Something called conscience is also part of "I am" it's the same thing that tells us what is good and what is bad. If what I do, I can justify it to my own self as right, and then it can be nothing but right. You can question me by saying a murderer can think "I did what I wanted to do and its right thing to do" so how is he justified? See here, his conscience caught of the negative energies inside him. He knows he is wrong but his heart says what he did was the right thing to do. Our world is made up of black and white. Of negative and positive forces that balances the life forces around us. Without negative, we would have been living in paradise. So, the "I am" which made him commit the murder is in a way also a part of being in this universe. His role being of negative character! Negative people like that are everywhere, they will pull you down, bully you, rebuke you, make you question your worth and threaten your "I am". It's how you maintain or select being good or bad, how you let these negative forces affect you, and transform you every day that is important. Remember who you are is not or will not be decided by them. You are and say with me "'I am" the sole creator of myself'. In the same way you are responsible to the way you play your role in this universe.

Evolution and Its Role in Changing the Identity of Humans:

As humans we evolve constantly, history shows us that we evolved from mainly primates of Africa, some 6-8 million years ago. We have grown so much from then to here. Not only our look, appearances, characteristics and behavior has changed over the years, but we have embraced some other aspects that made us who we are today. We learnt to walk on two legs, the complex structure and intelligence of our brain changed, we learnt the usage of different tools that eventually made us make machines of different types, language evolved and we learnt better to communicate not just with gestures but also with eyes, and complex things like telepathy. Art, cultural diversity, freedom of speech, law order, and science all came along gradually. We are not anymore, those furry creatures running from tree to tree eating raw. We know how to cook, how to socialize, how to decorate, how to beautify, how to appreciate, accept and grow. The identity of 'I' starts as you gain consciousness with your birth and much before you realize, the assimilation of it has begun. A part of' I 'is delivered with you at birth and the rest of it evolves as a person starts putting layers of learning of different kinds, creating moments with people around you which accumulate in your mind as memories and slowly make you into what you think you stand to be. Just like the process of human evolution goes through a series of changes – maybe the genetic set up, changes in representation of genes etc. giving rise to the finally evolved species in tandem with environmental factors too. Similarly, the 'I' is a product of changes in a person from birth to the phase where the identity is almost evolved. This may include simple things like a child initiated into a home where questioning and curiosity is rewarded and encouraged, eventually projects a human with an open mind and the need to know, an important trait in any identity. 'I am' is a combined product of a lot of things. I become a product of all that it has seen, felt and known. I could almost compare it to a tempting bowl of fruit salad…well; you take the bowl, that's you. Then add the fruits you would like to have in it, choose them, chop and mix them and add the seasoning of your choices and you have an inviting bowl of fruit salad and that's your identity!! The only difference being that the evolution of your identity has certain factors beyond your control like the circumstances provided by your life, your reaction to them and even your learning out of it!!

Changes in Identity of the Concept of 'I' As We Grow Biologically:

Are you the same person, you were when you were a rebellious teenager? Or even close to what you were a few years ago? Would you have taken the same decisions then that you think you would or should have taken now, given a chance to re live those moments? As we grow, both physically and mentally some things change the way we act or behave in society. Genetics does have a unique role in playing to your behavior pattern, but it has been proved time and again that we are much more than just what our genes make us to be. Researches over the years have shown that environment seem to play a bigger role than our actual genome. Even if the genetic makeup of an individual is predisposed to certain traits and as the individual grows the environment around does not support it then the trait is subdued immaterial of how strong it is!!! Some would even say astrologically identical people born in the same astrological sign would behave similarly, yet how far that's true is left to our imagination. The environment to which you grew up surely shaped and molded you to what you are today. And guardians or parents, teachers, friends are also important people who have shaped you to what you are today. Our memories play an important role in defining us. They sometimes encourage, sometimes discourage to act in a certain way and establish your "I am". Say you meet with a kind act when you were a child. Somebody bought you a cake free of cost in a shop on your birthday when you couldn't pay. That is a positive memory that will stay in your heart forever! You may end up doing the same for an orphan some day and bring a smile to an innocent face. Your brother got killed by a drunk driver when you were three. Not only this memory will not ever let you drink and drive, it can also make you a successful lawyer fighting DUI, DWI cases. See memories mold us into the beings we are now; and help us create a different form of "I am", and you change according to them. It differs from person to person how the memories will affect a person's behavior pattern. Somebody can opt for suicide after being raped; that memory lingering traumatically to one's brain.

Again, someone can get healed with the strength of "I am" power and become a social activist fighting with the government and supporting rape victims and counselling them for a better life. "I am" eventually means what I am, what I am capable of, what I am willing to do, what I am doing now!

We all walk the road of discovery, sometimes as a challenge and sometimes unknowingly to know who we are. For few the journey is easy and for some quite a task depending on the awareness of each individual. When you justify, you see in the mirror, the unrest somewhere within you falls and you descend to a level of peace. When this stage is arrived at, not many things outside you then can disturb the equilibrium and create any kind of chaos or confusion to your identity, since you acknowledge the identity to be the closest to what you wanted to be. This has been the path taken to reach the realization of you and therefore needs no explanation to the outside world.

"There are three things in the make- up of man -the body, the mind and the soul."- Vivekananda

We come with the body, the mind lives the moments and creates the memories and the soul is the choices we make in our lives.

Role of Memory in Creating the New "I "& The Power Of "I Am"

A huge part of our identity is created by memories and their reflections. Identity, in this, case is a linked chain whose links are the memories of your childhood, teenage and adulthood, carried in your mind as a continuous process. We go through enormous amount of changes and evolution every day. Not only during different phases in life and the decisions we take, but even in the mere daily cycle of everyday life. As we walk the life, our steps are decided by our previous experiences. We make our choices based on previous learning. There always exist some parts of life though, which remain unknown to us, and yet we move on hoping the pieces of puzzle will fit in.

We all live our lives as a part of a much larger universe. Each and every being here is connected to each other. There is one understanding we need to have at this point that there is only one universe, one reality and just one existent truth of our life...Quantum Physics brings forth the explanation that everything in the universe, that all form of matter- whether it is you or it is an inanimate object, is made of energy. But it is only a certain amount of energy or bit of energy called Quanta. Hence even our reality is made up of 'quanta' of energy. This energy exchange or interchange between matters creates our reality. We are all parts of this Universe, or rather different forms of the same ultimate energy. So our existence is simultaneous and in same period. There are no distinctions here, except the illusion created by our omnipresent ego and the interface of our senses involved in creating a reality. There are no separate identities as such; our related experience gives us the identity.

We are all a part of one system which encompasses all, and our co- existence occurs due to related energy interactions. Quantum physics also elaborates that anything exists because our thoughts brought about its manifestations. As we observe or think of something, the' quanta' join together to form various associations of atom and with the help of interpretation of our mind manifest into a physical reality. The same process forms the foundation of creating our reality and identity too. When we think of something, for example, a meeting with an old friend, the energy dynamics of it causes a reaction in the quantum field around us and as a result of that rearrange to produce either a thing or an experience for us. Since the bits of energy, quanta, are not bound by space or time, they have the power of being anywhere, anytime. They can only be influenced by other quanta.

Our reality, since it depends on energy exchange, keeps changing at any point of time. Our physical reality differs from our actual reality. Our present reality is our consciousness, with regard to the physical body whereas our actual reality refers to the infinite powerhouse of spiritual being. Each one of us is waiting to move towards our actual reality through our actions and thoughts. We are each waiting at the quantum door to open and we take a leap inside, through our choices and decisions in life. Each choice creates chain of memories which effectively create the "I ".

Believe In the Power of I Am

We perceive ourselves, with respect to the world, from two broad perspectives. One is just your own existence and its functionality, the other being the larger overall view of your existence in relation to the entire universe and the Supreme Being. Our aim in life is to travel the journey from just "I" towards a more open and vast consciousness of self in relation to the universe. The travel to enlighten the self or a stronger human being has to be a conscious effort. Once we are able to tap the inner power, our life immediately becomes simpler, more liberating and peaceful.

The infinity of 'I' shows us the power of self or the transformations it can bring about in an individual. Help him rise beyond life situations if need be and also to motivate self in case, where the self itself has created limitations by imposing self belief which may be negative in nature. The 'I am' has the power of connecting to the Supreme Being which does not reside anywhere else but within you. If we start believing in self and its energy, it can reverse the 'I can't 'to 'I can'.

The sun, situated in one place, illuminates the entire universe; so a small particle of spirit (the soul within the heart) illuminates the entire body with consciousness. Use the power of your soul to guide you to your destination.

Begin your days by deciding what you will add after 'I am' as, it is going to bring the reality you choose. As what you add after I am becomes your reality that is solely your own creation. If you harp on the fact that "I am incapable, I am unworthy, I am unlovable", and so on...that is going to become your fate. Trust in the powers inside of you. Dig out the true potential, try your best, give in with everything you have, even after that if something doesn't happen the way you planned, at least then you can blame the outside forces and feel good about yourself that you tried. The best part of human life is that you can choose your 'I am'. Our tongue through its words has the power to influence our life, so use the words wisely. What follows I am, unravels your reality, so choose it well. Invite good things in life and they will be given by God. If you start believing that you are unique and you are a masterpiece created by the divine, you will start feeling and being treated like one. Observe in your mind and it shall manifest itself. Shake off the negatives and the doubts you hold in your mind and you shall reach the destination decided for you.

"I am" is your true being; it's what your nature and potential is. You alone can say "I am" and no one else can do it for you. And when you say "I am" you are recognizing and establishing the presence of a holy spirit inside of you, that guides you into believing and achieving what you desire to be. It's like a door to your consciousness, of expressing yourself. When you try to establish something outside yourself, you cannot achieve it properly because your inner self does not agree with it. Say you have to work as a teacher, that's the only option available giving regards to the priorities in life and the circumstances available. You can never excel in teaching job as it's not what your heart tries to do. In your heart you know it's not true that you are a great teacher. You are robbing yourself of the opportunities that you can explore with your talents and making the poor students suffer who deserved a person who could have been a better teacher. One's mental attitude towards life and towards the situations that come in his way is crucial in shaping up his destiny. Do not ever say "I am not...". Always say and feel the opposite and challenge your inner powers. The only competition you should have is with you that were yesterday.

. Changing your "I am "may seem a tedious task yet it does not seem so, since it is you on whom is banks as to how quickly a particular aspect about your own self can change. The environment you are provided with and your motivational level in wanting to bring the change about can make it happen as per your desire. The tools which are used in the field like methodology of NLP makes it pertinent to let changes manifest much faster than we imagine. Sandra lost her mother in a car accident who was her only parent, along with getting jilted in love by her boyfriend that she felt her life just shattered. She entered into depression and had to rely on antidepressants daily. Her friend introduced her to a holistic living class and along with support at work and a great friend circle that she bounced back to life. She now truly believes that she alone has the power to control her life's course, and if you believe something passionately and give in all your strength to achieve it, nothing is impossible. Your world is your consciousness objectified. Bring change from within so your expressions outside along with your outlook will be fall in track themselves. Be the change you want to see in others. Keep complimenting and praising yourself for every little achievement. If you rise in your own eyes, nothing can be more rewarding that that. Strengthen the positive attributes of your mind, believe in them and strengthen them, harness them to be used as weapons to slay the negatives that come your way from outside. Take small steps but teach your body and its self to accept the unlimited power of your inner self, your spirit and the things you place in your thoughts and imaginations can become true for you! Believe to achieve!!!

CHAPTER 2: THOUGHTS AND BELIEFS:

Origin of Thoughts:

Our mind has the power to shape something in reality, if we are able to match the frequency of the reality to its energy. This is why we are often told - we are a sum total of energy or products of our mind or the thoughts we produce. And hence we become what we think. If this was so easy, then why in this world of innumerable opportunities, so many people are suffering? Why do we have people who are unhappy, unsuccessful and frustrated?? Why is it that there exists a gap between people's intention to succeed and actual success? The reason may lie in few interconnected thoughts – conformity, our model of reality ie, our beliefs and limited use of our power of mind & thoughts!!

What are thoughts? Where do they come from? What do they do? Can they be changed or altered? Too many questions, is it!! Well, let's find few answers too. How do I know "I am"? My mind tells me of my existence and my present being as a human. Mind is the generator of thought and also organizes them into ideas. Hence, we define a thought as the product of mental activity resulting in it. Neurologically a lot of chemical alterations make such things happen. This is something as fundamental to our existence as eating food for survival. Thinking happens consciously and unconsciously, with our permission and without it too. If the body starves, it would collapse, and the basic organs would stop functioning, which indirectly will alter the working of the brain too. The mind unable to do its primary function will get sick. Our existence is impossible without thinking, as it gives us the soul which makes us different from inanimate objects. All our actions are related to our thought process and without it we would simply be in a state of coma or cerebral palsy.

The process of a thought formation is done by mind. Neurons or the nerve cells in the brain are the main aspect of it, if we go into the biological aspect. The nervous system with its mother organ, the brain is behind the origin of thought. Thoughts are produced due to a stimulus. Sometimes the stimulus is consciously provided or sometimes it's picked up from our surroundings, without our knowledge. Thinking happens when we are awake and also when we are asleep. Brain is functioning all the time, involuntarily. As we grow beyond the basic origin of thought, the environment and its interactions with brain play a major role in growing years of life. When we see things around us, we assimilate them and make our own perceptions of it. The brain accommodates these in itself for further processing. These perceptions then command or control our actions. So how we think and what we do is all co-related.

The power of thought process or you can say stream line of consciousness is way beyond than can be fully understood. One string of thought leads to another. It takes immense practice and meditation to free your mind of thoughts and be blank. As if you have attained a state of "Nirvana" (a concept in Buddhist philosophy- where you go in a transcendent state far away from sense of real life, its materialistic importance, desire, hunger, suffering and sense of living as a human being on earth). This practice of shutting off thoughts for a few minutes in a day can greatly enhance our concentration power, balance of life and bring upon us, an immense state of calm.

Thoughts Create Our World & Belief System:

Everything that we understand, and live in this physical world, has an underlying explanation in our thoughts process. This inner world of thoughts and beliefs somewhere has to be understood and mastered if we were to have a hand in our destiny. Destinies aren't determined by spiritual powers alone. It also depends to a large extent what we think and the kind of thoughts that we attract. We build our own destiny, our mindset, beliefs and thoughts regarding our self, our inner strength make us what we are.

Just like we breathe without being conscious, same is with mind. It produces thoughts on its own accord. We end up acknowledging a few and we are unaware of a few. How a single thought is a basis of foundation of our world, more or less our existence itself is a question that can appear to many. It may not be a single thought but all our actions are guided by thoughts. And a single thought can alter a life changing decision or action which can be a total turning point of our life. This is how we act and behave. One after the other, thoughts bring a ripple of "how", "when", "why", and "what" in our minds. This chain of thoughts is the genesis of our beliefs; our very own belief system.

What is a belief? We can simply put it as a relationship about an experience. What we feel, what we see, what we encounter, gives us experience, and these experiences makes an opinion about matters in our mind. These opinions create a belief about something which is a bit difficult to change as it has developed from things that has happened to us. Every thought or opinion that we form in our minds are not belief. There may be thousands of thoughts in mind but only few become beliefs. Beliefs are those thoughts that your mind starts believing as real because of your experiences and emotions attached to them. Our beliefs are our personal laws created as we grow, to make the reality of our lives. They could be called as our guiding principles which are ingrained in our subconscious mind. These create our reality. You and I may differ in the set of beliefs we hold and that's precisely how our realities shape up differently. Our perception of reality differs since our belief systems have developed with different inputs. Thoughts lead to actions; actions in turn lead to results. Results may be positive or negative as per our actions and circumstances. If we get a positive result, it leads the mind to accept it as a belief and encourages similar actions and behavior later based on that belief. A person then follows this cycle again and again repeatedly in mind often unconsciously to form a mindset or a pattern in which it would work in a given set of circumstances. Anna, a 3 year old is a surprisingly sharing child. She was told by her parents as she grew up and started having peer playing that if she shared her toys, she in turn would get to play with others toys too. If others see her sharing they too will share their toys with her. The parents encouraged her actions with a positive pat and an occasional treat for the same. It soon became her mindset and belief that sharing is good.

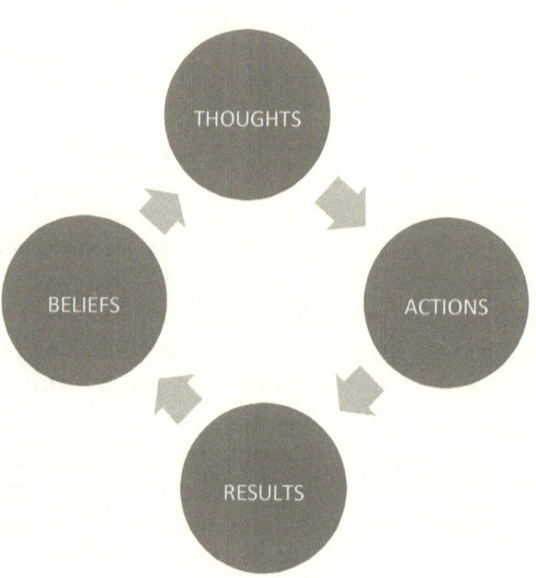

We would hence describe a mindset as a set of beliefs that decide how we behave or what our attitude is towards life or things around us. The mindset can be positive or negative depending on life situations that made it.

The human dilemma of being caught in one's mind gets reflected when we do not want to die for a belief because we may be wrong. Many a time, our life experiences come to unpleasant conclusions. Does that mean that the second time it still would be the same? No, it has a possibility of changing. See when a situation changes, the people who enacted a part in the first half also changes, perspectives, actions, environment, circumstances, all change. So eventually the results will not be same. But when we face a situation in life that connects us emotionally and alters our thought process to a large extent, we make an opinion out of it. We strongly believe that if 2+3=5 and somehow cannot accept that 1+4 can also be 5. I might be wrong, is something that most of us do not want to believe. The supreme "I" is always right. Our belief system is thus shaped by the thoughts we pet in our minds which is again a result of a number of permutations and combinations of environmental and social factors around us. It creates a world in which we snug in to live as we are comfortable to think matters that way and gives us a world created by our own.

When we sometimes peep into our belief system due to certain circumstances we have been put in we have to evaluate whether our belief system is empowering or hindering. This may reflect why we stand were we do, in our lives? If it is empowering we see success in our lives. if we seem to put in our best and still do not meet success then we question our belief which may be hindering our results. It now occurs to us that our subconscious always plays a part in delivering our beliefs and hence should be kept in mind. The unlimited power of mind is not tested to its core and left underutilized. We seem to conform to societal norms, of what may be others expect us to do and lead a life not exactly as you portray it to be. We end up believing that our life shaped up the way it is because of external factors. Factors way beyond our control, whereas the truth is that we are what we are because of what our original thoughts were.

Challenging the Belief System:

Our mind is like a fertile land. It produces what seeds have been sown into it. Human mind has riches way beyond anybody's imagination and can reap dividends beyond our expectation. The catch here is to control what we sow. we control our thoughts and our actions can be controlled. Hence, we control how our lives shape up. If we can alter our attitudes in life we can alter our life too.

When a person believing by what he is capable of realizes that his potential is not reached, starts doubting his capability and also his belief system. These moments can sometimes really pull you down in the sand with having no control of stopping it. How do we then analyze such state of existence and stand back up? We need to check our thoughts; we analyze our actions and the attitude behind them, our efforts and then see the results. We generally do not challenge our own belief system because we ourselves have validated it and made it true. It's not easy to validate those beliefs. Since we hold them true it starts to define us. We somewhere need to stop defining ourselves through the belief and stop identifying with it. Many times, what we believe can be wrong, but facts in life may not be so. When we come around to doing the same thing again, it means we are stuck in a life situation beyond our control. We need to re-assess our beliefs in those cases and try to change. We need to check the validity of the belief, whether it holds true only for us or it's a universal truth, whether it held true in a similar situation in others life or not? When the answers come rolling in us we realize those times has changed and it's time for the belief to renew and change as per the need of the hour. It takes time to admit ourselves to such changes.

Grandma may have lived a life where women's life centered on kids and kitchen and family life. She may find this is the best for any ideal family as she has nurtured this core belief system for long and also have seen examples of woman making their home heaven for her kids and husband like these for ages. However, times have changed. She may not like the current lady of the house go out work with men, and keep the kids in crèche, as this will question her inner belief system. She needs to understand assimilate and change her belief system as per changing times, and accept that men and women are equally responsible for the tasks at home and in matters of children. This is what changing times have brought upon us, and for her its challenging her belief system to accept new ways of living and adjusting.

When we realize that our belief system has started limiting us we need to control the steering wheel of our mind. Would it not be fantastic to imagine the mind equal to a machine with you at the steering wheel, than your hands folded and the machine moving into a pit. If you direct it with a worthwhile purpose it moves in a determined manner to its destination. It will take you to success you deserve. From our childhood our belief system shape and mold our character. They become a part of our character and we do not realize how they affect our perceptions and reactions. Whenever we do not like something around us; it's our beliefs that negatively self talk into our minds and make assumptions based on that. They may be wrong, but they make our attitude and behavior in life. Suppose you have seen your parents bring you up with the belief that it's good to make everyone happy. It's true and very much appreciated? But what if someone takes this attitude of yours for granted and takes advantage of it and makes you feel worthless? Would you please the wrong person just to stick to the belief you have grown up with? NO! It brings heartache, failure and bad self esteem and those beliefs should be changed or preserved for someone better. We want our efforts be appreciated by others, we feel good about it. However, it doesn't matter if one person rejects you or finds fault in you. He cannot be the sole judge of your worth. Everyone has self respect and dignity and that need not be stamped by someone who looks down upon you. Get in touch with positive inspiring people, think well about yourself, shoot the goal of your life with all the passion you have, and see your dreams come true!

Fear of Rejection Limiting Beliefs:

Whenever we face situations where all factors influencing it are not known we develop a sense of fear in facing it. Sometimes certain beliefs of ours are baseless or false and hence lead us to situations which put fear and a sense of rejection into us. Negative influences in our life make us question our worth. It may be done by bullying siblings, wrong parenting, or pressure of environment you grew up with. We end up 'believing' that we are worthless, "I cannot do it", "I am not worthy or it", "I am not good enough" are words that you often end up mumbling to yourself. The negative influences have harmed our belief system, and we are glued to it even if it's not true. We are scared to take a risk, plunge into the unknown, and see the other side of the rainbow as we fear unknown. We are afraid to walk into those lanes as our experiences have never encouraged exploring. We fear that our efforts will be rejected, and thus proving our worthless identity to which, we do not want another stamp.

Conditioning fear is another way that limits possibilities. We may stay calm, put our chin up and prepare for the best. But when the situation to present ourselves appear, boom! The fear comes back again. It's difficult to challenge our beliefs about rejection and criticism and stand tall. We are so conditioned by negative influences that we have become dependent on it. We constantly think unconsciously "what will others think?" Ask yourself this… why do you need to prove yourself to others? Just give your best and let situation take care of the rest. What has to happen will happen, and biting nails, tearing hair and sweating palms about it will not help in any way. Even if you get rejected at one thing doesn't mean you are a failure. It just means that thing was not good enough to test your true spirit. Try better next time, getting over the fear of rejection, and just play the game. You will definitely win. Living in fear is not pleasant, and a fearless heart has a long way to go.

Take an example of Adam, a 14 year old teenager, always anxious in class or elsewhere about how he stood in a group. His surroundings of bully groups or over expectation of his parents may have made him that way. However, it became very important for him to prove himself. Even in a playground with kids playing football, his performance was so important to him it almost felt like a life and death situation inducing tremendous amount of anxiety. As he progressed into teenage where relationships where surfacing with the other gender his anxiety got the better of him before he could even break the ice. In depth understanding of his happenings revealed links of past when he was a preschooler. With working parents and a special child as a sibling to take care of, Adam always got a no as an answer whether he asked for something. He was constantly limited in his efforts and performances and made to understand his responsibilities as an elder. When he asked his mates of class over to come over to study together, his offer was rejected because he had a younger brother who they thought intimidated them. This was far from reality. Rejection at these junctures set a pattern in his mind, even as his identity was still evolving into a self defeating one for no faults of his. These kinds of incidents cause immense pressure on a mind. Say Adam who has faced rejections due to his younger brother can never feel like inviting his girlfriend for dinner, with the fear of rejection that his brother may intimidate her too! He will never plunge into asking her and his belief will limit his abilities to handle such situations.

The journey here begins with identifying the thought which goes against the person causing distress and negative emotions, and the false belief it has created in a mind. These thoughts need to be challenged and replaced with more realistic and balanced ones. Here in the example, Adam may get rejected by one girl, but he still has to try. All girls may not be the same, and one fine day he will find someone who can accept and admire his special brother and embrace him into their lives. Unless he tries to get over his fear of rejection and goes forward he will never know who or what is best for him.

Event: Refusal by mate of Adam

Belief: I am at fault; I am not accepted and not loved.

Consequences: Feeling of distress, hurt and overwhelming feeling of being alone, not finding future initiative to take a stand and proceed in life.

This framework is then challenged with question what does this mean for Adam, was he at fault, is it that big a reality that it should mar his identity? Slowly the process begins by changing the thoughts one by one. The fear of rejection can only be got over by taking the plunge. Once, twice, thrice he may fail, but trying to succeed will not only test his capabilities, but also give him perspectives in trying in different ways. Experiences and failures can only be a teacher to guide us into delivering our best and eventually succeed.

Practicing Critical Thinking To Change Existing Belief:

Once we are able to identify what limits belief, we can challenge them through critical thinking and overcome the same.

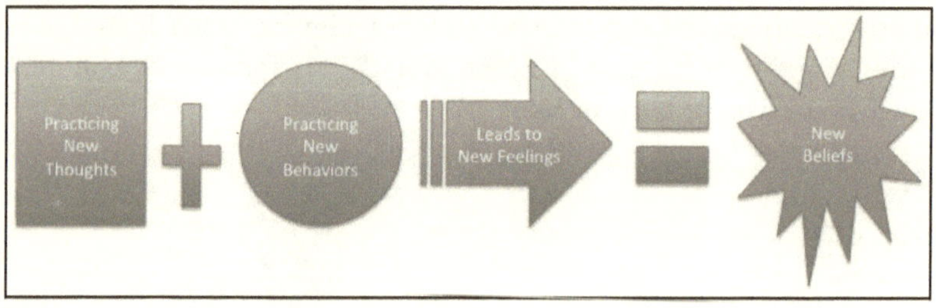

Critical thinking involves conscious action and a set or combination of skills to be developed. To be aware of one's self may be the first requirement on road to critical thinking. To be able to identify and accept the situation is the biggest obstacle to overcome. Being aware helps a lot in this. Then the need to overcome the emotional aspect of it comes to see it rationally. We ask questions and try at our level best to give the best possible answers. Complete truthfulness in these matters is of prime importance. An open minded attitude and being accepting even of unpleasant outcomes with the sole intention to overcome a strong belief may make all the difference. Complete discipline as an individual, as we go through the process of self identifying will eventually bring out the long ingrained sometimes wrong belief towards a more realistic one. The power resides in one's own mind it just needs to be unleashed. It takes time to cultivate an empowering belief after having slowly raised the older and redundant. The release an individual goes through as it happens is phenomenal. Almost as a sunrise after challenging days of not seeing a sun in winter!! Better and improved life waits for each who has the will.

Identifying a core belief than that of reality is the first step to solving the mysteries of the mind. Changing our attitude towards our self, changes the thoughts that long dominated us. Instead of the belief system to do the thinking for us, let's think rationally using our brain. Ask questions; challenge what was told to you or what others thought about you. When our thought process about our self changes; our attitude towards life and behavior pattern also changes. When our behavior towards a given subject or matter changes, the actions we took earlier in the same matter will also change. And when we change our actions and do not repeat what we earlier did based on our beliefs, results will also change.

Suppose we are afraid of public speaking. It is a fear that has long been ingrained inside us. No matter how much we practice in front of the mirror, when we see crowds and faces in front us, we start to panic. It's a fear where we get conscious of what others will think of us? "What if I forget a line?", "What if they laugh at my points?", "What if I am questioned for which I don't have any answer?" these all may intrigue us to not give our best and hence confirming the belief that "I cannot speak in public". This same logic applies when it comes to asking someone for date, asking for leave in office or an appraisal, or asking for our rights! Apply critical thinking, switch off the lights in the audience and see the difference. It will be the same as speaking in front of the mirror. A newly found self confidence can be assured and the result will be different.

Be curious; ask questions about yourselves, surroundings, your core beliefs, and what others think about you. Seek for information and evidence to matters of your belief. "Is it what "I" think of myself? Or is it what I think about myself because someone else thought about me in that manner? "Do not blindly follow what everyone feels about you. You are closest one to yourself. If you do not think well about you, that will get transmitted to others and hence the same attitude will be reflected by them. Be open to new in formations and using them to change your inbuilt perspectives. Finally having humility to accept that you were wrong about yourself and be open to new ideas and evidences that prove your worth. Do not flow with the current and go to unwanted destinations, make the current flow with you and reach your goals!

Laws of Attraction:

When we are able to change the set of beliefs which limit us , we realize suddenly that we become much more luckier than we ever thought ourselves to be!! Really do we actually become lucky or we start attracting things more positively with our own positive mindset.

Everything in the physical universe is made of energy and its vibrations. Hence if we send out positive energy we seem to attract the same.

How Do We Become Proactive In Executing This Law Of Attraction?

- We control our thoughts- with simple process of eliminating any negative aspect which may enter your mind. Just stop sending the wrong thoughts.

- Get over self-imposed limitations on your mind and let it soar to new heights with the wings it always had.

- Have the courage to have a concrete goal and stand by it. Imagine all the ways to reach the same and refuse to believe that anything can stop you in achieving it.

- Make your mind believe that the success beliefs it holds are from your own experiences. They give you the confidence that you already have things in life that you should be happy about.

- Repeat to your subconscious mind the visualized goal and imprint it. The thoughts which we then send out are more in sync with our goals. This synchronizes with vibrations in the universe drawing similar ones to it.

It may be a wrong perception which makes us believe that harder we work the more successful we become. It is the way your thoughts work, that can turn around your destiny.

Attitudes, Values and Beliefs:

For a person to acknowledge how his mind works and how he behaves are all interlinked and related to each other. Attitudes are simply likes and dislikes of a person; they are hypothetical assumptions of an experienced mind. These are those experiences that he grew up with, and situations to which he was exposed in the past. Attitudes represent our judgment towards a situation, a person or a thing. They could be positive, negative or ambivalent. These attitudes stem from our inner framework or grid of beliefs that are developed over time. The main aspects considered in the evolution of an attitude are the emotions which appear during a situation, behavior and thoughts. The interactions of these are displayed in an attitude.

As we live our lives and play out the different roles that are handed over to us there is continuous interaction of our inner framework with that of others. All our interactions are validated by how we collaborate with other people holding other belief systems and values. It is hence seen we get drawn to people who share our core values and become more compatible towards them. That may be educational, social, career or relationships. In our lives we come across people, who have the knowledge and the skills to do any task, they execute everything with a positive attitude. We tend to copy what we believe is better than us. Say you love street shopping, but in office you come across a person and share cubicle with him who is extremely brand conscious. You can see the hatred in his eyes about people who shop from the streets. Not only will you hide the fact that you love to bargain and shop from the street but will also develop a habit of getting influenced by his views and start shopping from big brands. Our behavior or what actions we take are generally ruled by what we think, our beliefs, and the values inculcated because of them and hence our attitudes reflected in them.

Issues arise when the attitude takes a negative note or the ability to express or indulge in right behavior is not there in a person and hence the person being labeled as a person with undesirable attitude. This may need attitude realignment by feedback in changing behavior in this context. Once the behavior pattern changes, there is a change in belief system too. To be able to manage and regulate these, helps in overall understanding of personal management and brings about reaching maximum potential of a person.

Origin Of Thoughts And How They Shape Our Reality:

It's very simple to answer that our thoughts originate in our brains. But it is not true. It originates outside our brain, what we see, what we feel, what are being taught and told us about, what value system are we raised up with; what kind of person we are in society, and what challenges brings out from the mind of us. Your brain does not create thoughts, it assimilates information and knowledge that we absorb every day and processes them to our abilities to understand a situation and command and function accordingly. From the time we are exposed to information and knowledge or any outside view through using our five senses, to assimilation, processing and acting upon it, there are mainly three stages.

What we are born with, or our genetic makeup is very important to us. We do inherit certain traits from our parents, but we evolve according to our environment. Our behavior and our related biology seems more in tandem with our environment than the disposition of genes. Core values evolve as we grow and with the experiences we seem to have in life. Even twins having the same DNA will not react to a similar situation identically. This is called individuality and potential that varies from person to person. Next stage is level of understanding and capability to react to a given situation. A first-time mother may get irritated with consistent crying of her new born and feel frustrated about it. Another mother may try to keep calm and understand why the child crying is and find an appropriate solution to it. Both are faced with similar situations but how differently they react to both cases depends on their level of understanding. We analyze what we receive and transform it into thoughts and concepts about a particular matter. Third is the ability to realize what actions need to be done when we meet new circumstances. In the example above the mother can try to feed the baby, try finding solutions like whether her diaper is full or having gas troubles or feeling sleepy. It is the action that she needs to take and her motherly thoughts would best understand that and take care of the reality- in this case crying.

We can argue from where does an idea or thought "pop" into our head. Say you are having dinner with colleagues in a restaurant and suddenly you remember you haven't spoken to your mother for a week. This is definitely a thought. But where did it originate from? You did not see her picture, you were not discussing mothers, you did not smell her favorite perfume, or taste a pie that was her specialty. Then why did the thought come over? Subconscious mind is a part of mind which is not your conscious mind, not presently 'there' with you, but stored somewhere deep inside your brain. It stores all your pasts, your beliefs, your feelings, memories, skills, whatever you have seen, and things you have felt. Realty is having dinner with colleagues, but it was shaped into remembering to call your mother by a stray thought that rose from your subconscious of not interacting with her for long. Our brain is a complex organ, and there is no valid reason for the ways it behaves.

Our life changes and differs from others because of our thought processes. Our thoughts create our reality. How do we create our life is entirely dependent on our thoughts? It may seem funny because outside factors play important roles in life and it's not entirely dependent on our mentality. There may be birth defects, there may be natural catastrophes, there may be parenting issues, role of our oppressors, a life altering illness etc. that totally changes our thoughts from what we have grown up with or seen around us. We constantly change our thoughts and beliefs according to change in life situations. Have you ever thought about your leg being the most important part of your body? Not, really right? You can come up with options like hands eyes or brain having superior priority over other body parts like a leg. But ask somebody who had a road accident and lost a leg. How does that person feel? How this change of events in his life, changed his perspectives and thoughts and now for him a leg is the most important part of his body that he lost. His thoughts about importance of body parts have changed forever, and his realty is that he has lost his leg, which is most dear to him now.

Every aspect of a person's life, his relationships, work, finances, and health, lifestyle reflect his thoughts which are always subject to changes with outside force. And the power of thoughts is limitless!!! Every decision you make, every step you take, you are a cocoon inside your thoughts that are rightly spun around your consciousness and sub consciousness making you a creator of your own destiny, of your own life!

CHAPTER 3: SUFFERING THE EGO:

What Is Ego?

What exactly is Ego? It is defined as the "I" or self of a person. It is this sense of self which interacts with the environment and the people in society. It is a superior feeling and esteem of one's self, and its importance. It distinguishes the self of a person from his own point of view to other's self. The term ego sees its origin in Germany in the year 1780-1790. It not only explains our consciousness of our identity with the subconscious it constantly toggles between the two to represent a picture of our self that we present to the rest of the world.

Ego is not something that we acquire by doing something great in life, or being beautiful, rick or popular. Of course, these may be the reasons that fan the egoistic self of our nature, but ego is something we are born with. Even we can say an unborn child in a mother's womb has ego. We can say, ego is a self-defense mechanism that naturally originates within us to fit in the roles that are given to us. We do not want to stay behind in any race, and if not the world, to us we appear superior. If somebody doesn't praise us for some good that we do, we do rarely think that the fault was in us. We blame the other person for not having the right eyes to appreciate brilliance. That's a sense of ego that we cultivate in our self-long before we even meet this world and face its challenges. There is always the survival of the fittest. So, in order to fit in, we create a false sense of identity of our self, as something great, in order to survive. Say we have a physical body that brings along with a shadow. Think of the sun as the adversities and oppositions in life. The more the heat of the sun is there, stronger or blacker the shadow will be. Same is with ego, when faced with adversities, and challenges, our ego takes the stand to protect us in our subconscious way and is stronger than ever. However, when the sun is mild, the shadow is mild too; same is the situation with ego. Whatever the exterior situation is, accordingly our ego will be strong or weak.

From the time we are born, we see, we hear, we feel and make conclusions about the physical world around us. We hear sounds but cannot differentiate into words. The most soothing sound seems to come from a figure whose way of talking is long known, soon we learn to call that person "mommy". Till now everything comes as different objects, but we stand strong to our likes and dislikes, of faces, of hunger, or being carried around, idea of being snug etc. as we concentrate on the words spoken to us, we slowly understand the meaning of "you", or "yourself" that eventually becomes, "me", and "myself". Children are often confused with their sense of self and often speak like this – "Ellie wants to have milk" instead of "I want to have milk". This sense of "I" and its importance takes time to settle in one self. She is told that the pink cup belongs to "you" and the blue cup to Peter. Frankly she will not be so heartbroken to find Peters cup to be broken, then if the pink cup breaks. It was "yours" and a part of her identity is lost. That what differentiated her from Peter is lost, and being a five year old, she will have no option but to cry her heart out till another pink cup arrives. Her ego will again be boosted, and she will feel herself in a comparable position with Peter about having a pink cup and feel good about it.

We are aware that all things around us, our self and our identity exist because of our inner realities or the grid of thoughts, beliefs and the value system developed from childhood. What we see of any person is their external picture, what lies beneath the external shield is convincingly covered with a layer of ego. Hurt that ego once and you can bring the worst of a person out. This needs to be overcome to see the inner truth of a person's existence since all actions and behavior are regulated by our core system of right and wrong from the beginning of our self. Hence in understanding our self we need to go beyond to what our mind tells us, with the interplay of ego working on it. Sometimes the ego blocks the understanding by creating illusions of self in mind. The first perception of "you" hides beneath a deeper human being who may be much more rational and meaningful. What does ego do? It can rule what a person understands and stop the discovery of the inner self. If we were to open the curtains of ego to decipher the play we would realize that it plays this role to keep only a superficial understanding of it to continue the external easy pretense. Ego makes us live in false belief if we are not guarded enough to see through. It lets a brother envy his little sister who's more accomplished in social life because of her talent. It may lead you to even be jealous of your workmate since he seems to rise the ladder of success faster than you could. It leads you to be deluded into the fact that your happiness and success is outside you, in others and their behavior and achievements. This is the farthest anyone could ever be from reality. It is in this manner that a person is held back in completing his journey towards his own realization of what he could be.

Is it possible to survive without ego in this world, if it is concerned to be such an obstacle in enabling our self discovery? If we were to move away from this view that ego is our enemy, and start believing that it is a part of our existence, and accordingly cope with it to discover peace within our self, that would be wonderful isn't it? It would enable us to experience life and hold the perspective that mind has a bigger power and reach and it can be more practical and logical. Going beyond the ego to find what's deeper inside us, should be the goal of our lives. Ego thinks about only himself, and heart (The true "I", me, the inner power, Connection to god, our heart) speaks about 'us', 'we', 'them'. Through self awareness, control of our thoughts, feelings, changing perspectives and behavior, and changing the way we speak to others can open the gates for the negative ego to go from us. We live in society where we live in extreme competition in every step. We use human ladders to reach success and further ego gets boosted. Ego holds our heart and our true potentials captive. It works in subconscious mind, so even when you are sleeping you dream of winning over a colleague of yours in office. In your heart you know that the person deserved the appraisal, but your ego binds and restricts your judgment by wishing bad luck to him. This is what we call our dark side. It's an integral part of our soul, same as good side. As the soul feeds the body, the ego feeds the soul. Ego is neither good nor bad, it is what we make out of it, and let which side of our nature to dominate our actions and behavior. Take the example of yin and yang. The voices of our inner self can be white spot in the yang, whereas ego can be said to be the dark dot in the light of yin. Both are required for the other to process. The ego that is burning you from the fact that your colleague got the appraisal and not you, can also bring something good from it. You may try even better from the previous times, succeed in your efforts and get your goal. Your ego was hurt and it made you do better! You wanted to establish your personal superior feeling of your identity and you did it! So, ego cannot be judged by what it holds in our heart, but what it makes us do in life.

Psychologically ego is seen as a facilitator of self. Psychoanalyst *Sigmund Freud* is of the opinion that ego is an important aspect of our existence. The ego is that part of us that prevents us from acting on our basic urges and helps us reach a balance. It is believed to be a link to the conscious as well as the unconscious part of our psyche. Hence understanding the working of ego as part of life conditioning may help us understand our framework better and work towards the universal truth. Sometimes it feels that ego may be omnipresent, in certain conditions it overpowers your thinking, rationality and knowledge and makes others believe that you are egocentric. It exists as a part of you and it remains up to you to either let it dominate or let it be dormant. All the pain and suffering is from the ego and not from outside or from superior powers above us. As we move from one stage of life to another our identity also keeps changing, it takes different shades with experiences as it meets. So let move beyond the thought that our sufferings and pain were written in our destiny. We are what we create and believe and as such it is our mind which brings our pain, doubts, hindrances and dilemmas, not sent by the Supreme Being. Critical thinking with the help of gathered knowledge frees us from the negative clutches of ego. Knowledge can only save one from getting overruled by ego problems.

Interplay of Belief System and Reasons for Emotional Sickness:

Beliefs constitute the base of our life, the mental land on which we live. All our conduct, including the intellectual life, depends on the system of our authentic beliefs. In them lies latent, as implications of whatever specifically we do or we think. This actually defines how ingrained a belief system is, in human mind because we use it to define our individual personal sense of reality and identity. The boundaries of our individual system are generally not defined and there are no clear-cut boundaries specified. All this is at war with our ego since somewhere the understanding of one helps assimilate the other.

What causes mental sickness? Is arrogance and insecurities anyway related to causing ego and therefore all the mental turmoil's that holds with it? Even after getting revenge to what we think was unfair to us, why don't we always get peace of mind? Why is there a sense of vacuum even after we reach our target that our ego decides for us? Our conscious and subconscious has important roles in playing its parts to questions like these. Even when our ego is satisfied, our heart not necessarily will. And it creates an itch, emptiness, a feeling of being incomplete. Is an arrogant man wrong? Arrogance is a quality often taken simultaneously with people who think of themselves as superior beings. However, this is just a variation of ego. A single person can have positive self-belief and negative self-belief at the same time, generally surfaced at different situations in life. Like the yin and yang both types of self-belief together form an ego. Sometimes they offset us into mentally being sick, somebody who has been subjected to bitter criticism and constant judgment may have negative self-belief. He will think of himself as worthless, and there his negative ego comes to play its part. He may try to live superior to others, proving others wrong about him may become his constant inner struggle. He may even resort to pulling someone down to go up in the ladder. He wears a mask of superiority and confidence, but his inner heart remembers all those criticism and judgment and this offsets his emotional balance. He will feel sick, unsatisfied and constantly suffering from self-analysis. When confidence gets into the head of a person his actions are based on assumptions that his arrogance offers him with. Being not defensive or sharp and being humble can may a times be branded as inefficient, lack luster and shy. He will feel insecure and try to fight back. However, this is not required. What is most important is what he thinks of himself. Having confidence over arrogance, being humble over insecure can give pathways that destroy the positive and negative self-images of ego.

Pain and Suffering in Human Life - "It's Your Belief" Change It, It Will Change Your Personality:

Pain is a physical sensation which the mind and body feels. It's rather the mind tells the body to acknowledge the feeling of pain and experience it as a result of some injury which is accidental or inflicted due to a reason. Suffering and pain though are always spoken of together in the same breath, are uniquely different stand apart. Pain can be inevitable in certain circumstances like getting stitches on a gash. It can be self-inflicted pain too which obviously is not inevitable. Suffering is an optional feeling. You can opt to suffer or not decide to do so. Pain can be physical or mental. When you get hurt mentally that causes much more pain than a physical pain. Mental pain sometimes takes years to get well, whereas physical pain just days or months. Suffering is related mentally than physically. A person in coma has no pain but he is suffering. Suffering also happens due to hurt ego. When yourself respect feels threatened by outside forces your negative ego gets agitated. It looks for nooks and corners like a poked snake to lash out its venom. You have to change your belief system. You have to let go of things that bring the worst in you. You choose to suffer for someone who doesn't even deserve your worth. The fact that the person did not care about hurting your ego, means he/she doesn't have the same worth for you in their heart than you have in yours. So, if they can be so casual about hurting you, do not look back, call for the good in you and march forward!

Entering a doctor's office with a baby in arms for a vaccination always tells you that the baby will feel pain when the needle goes in. It is for the child's well-being; it hence should be dealt as a temporary pain for the child, by the mother. The mother on the other hand imagines this pain to be a suffering on her. It is completely a choice which can be avoided. Reason and question your core beliefs. Is she hurting her child intentionally? NO! Then the suffering she brings on herself has no logic. She should change her beliefs about the matter and make arrangements to see how fast the child can come out of the pain and be happy in her arms again.

Suffering has a different significance in life. It can be a temporary feeling due to some unpleasantness in a relationship or a broken relationship, a loss of parent and so on. It can remain for some time and can be overcome with better awareness of self. Memories can make you stronger. They are those aspects in life which no one can change. Negative ones can remain for longer to haunt you if not dealt at the self level. Who suffers actually? It is the 'I'. Suffering depends on how you perceive it, it may mean you being unhappy or tolerating pain

/dissatisfied feeling because of someone or something outside you. It may or may not involve pain. It may involve physical, emotional and mental pain. Reality of life states that whether t is pain or suffering, it cannot remain forever. It is temporary and hence should be treated so. Our wrong conditioning perhaps makes us believe that it will lost forever as our positive or negative ego is involved in it. It was not destined by the spirit in Universe. Let go of ego that causes you pain and suffering, with time, all wounds heal, whether they can be seen or felt. How you release your mind from the sufferings of ego is completely your call.

Our Emotions and Interplay of Ego:

Our emotions and our feelings play a important part in our lives, its share of pain and suffering. We know we feel but a lot of us do not know how to channelize feelings and how to process it? We get a great job offer, life feels good and we are happy. Even after getting something that we wanted for long we sometimes are unable to understand why we can't feel the happiness in it. Some feeling from past pops up to give us uneasiness; may be if you have got the job offer earlier you could have saved your father from dying!! This makes you feel run down, since the previous feeling has not been processed and moved out of system for no further reference. There are happy and sad feelings. We cannot just agree to feel the good ones and deny the sad ones because we do not like them. They even induce certain mental reactions because you have refreshed the same memory and the feeling with a similar situation. Our actions are swayed by feelings, emotions and sense of ego! The sooner we realize that, the better it works out for us. These stashed away feelings may dim a part of your own identity and you may start disconnecting with that aspect of yours. Lot of human suffering is due to emotions and feelings which have not been processed.

Emotions and ego are different sides of the same coin. Humans have two biggest possessions, emotions and intelligence. Rational thinking versus ego! However, a person may be intelligent when emotions comes to play, it overrules all logic. Emotions binds us, ego unleashes a part of our emotions that can be used destructively or constructively as per choice. The ego that is connected to one's spirituality can be more powerful than anything else. When we show emotions and ego to our parents, friends, spouse, it is different, much more worldly and sane. However, the emotions and ego that related and connected to our spiritual world can have unknown implications. Some of us believe in god, some of us do not. Bible says that we should not boast. Boasting is directly related to ego. To get in touch with your inner self, whether you believe in god or not, to trust in higher powers, you should let go of ego completely. Attain spiritual illumination, discover your true potentials by not wasting time in calculating who did what and not, and how can you go beyond. When you're true powers are unleashed and your emotions parallel to your ego, with no one dominating each other then only you can succeed in life.

Looking Beyond Distress:

It's in our hands to overcome the pain and suffering ego brings on to us during our lifetimes. It is the powerful mind which needs reconditioning to evolve and stand true to its desired destination. It needs intervention. The therapy we shall talk about forks on the fundamental understanding that humans react not just to event in the external environment but also interpret the reality with their understanding of beliefs of self and others. Rational emotive behavior therapy focuses on resolving emotional and behavioral problems and disturbances and lets them live a stress free and fulfilling life. This theory was developed by American psychologist *Albert Ellis.*

Rational Emotive Behavior Therapy:

This theory works on assumption that humans can be disturbed emotionally not just due to external agent but also due to their internal assimilation of thoughts through their beliefs. This framework assumes that humans have both innate rational (which mean constructive, self helping) and irrational (meaning self-destructive) tendencies. It claims that people to a large extent consciously or unconsciously make emotional difficulties like blaming self, hurt, getting anxious, giving in to ego demands, behaviors like avoidance, etc. This therapy is then applied as an educational process where the person in need of assistance is helped in identifying the self-defeating beliefs. Lot of questioning and reasoning follows and then the trait is replaced by a more self-helping one. The main aim of this theory is to show that if there are disturbing external events around the person, there is a choice of feeling the way you feel about yourself and changing that can change your life. This empowers the person to unlearn to be unhappy and learn again behavioral changes which help us become a happier person. The willingness to identify the issue and the determination to change the picture plays an important role here. Unless you admit there is an internal problem you will not seek help, and unless you seek help you cannot change, and unless you change, the same psychological issues which caused you hurt, pain suffering and anxiety will not resolve.

Wake Up The Real 'You':

Why is it sometimes we feel despondent, we suffer from hurt and anger and we end up asking *'why me'*? Somewhere along the line we have accumulated a lot of clutter and may be unwanted need and desires that we don't want and never stood true to our real nature!! In trying to resolve and attain many of these desires we alienated ourselves from the real 'we' and fell in the trap to become someone else. We always aspire to copy and be someone else, a better cook, a better singer, a better entrepreneur, and in the process lose out on our own capabilities, talents and powers. You cannot be a good singer, but you can be a better painter! Understand and seek what is your hidden talent, what are the things that you are good in? Ask people to list down 5 different good points about yourself and 5 bad points about you. You will be amazed at your result. If you see more people have a common bad remark like "arrogant" you know you have to change that trait as most feel like that about you. By doing this exercise you will find answers to your 'good' sides too, how you can use them as swords to defeat what has been listed as bad about you.

At this juncture we have two options. One is to go on the same road which takes you away from your own self misguiding your mind creating a false self-identity about yourself. The other option is to realize we made a mistake n our understanding and hence realign back to the path which takes you to a more better you. Suppose you feel you have high opinions about yourself having good looks, and your ego just doesn't get satisfied enough when you look at the mirror many times of the day. But when you get the result, you see that most people have not written anything about your good looks and focused on things like "kind hearted person". You should use this as an opportunity to enhance this kind heart of yours to bring more peace of mind. We are human and like they say we are bound to make mistakes. Yet if we have the conviction to get back up the war is not lost yet. The journey may not sound so simple, does not feel easy as you decide to step on unknown paths of your character. Complete dedication, humility and focus towards your goal will resurrect your own self from the shadows of your ego.

Your belief system and understanding the virtues of yourself:

As individual sometimes we are not aware of our own belief system completely and get influenced by what others think or believe about us. The belief system itself stands in your way in not letting you reach where you desire to be. Somewhere the realization has to dawn on you that besides what is known consciously there are a lot of things which rule our subconscious mind and are almost not known to us. We see what we want to see, we hear what we want to hear and we feel what we want to feel. Supposing a person wants to avoid you, but being nice, he keeps on taking your calls and telling you he is busy so please call him later. You want to *hear* that you are important to him and he just doesn't have time, so will take your call eventually someday. But what you can't *listen* to is that he does not want to get your calls, and just wants you to understand that at your own time.

A doctor gets a call that he has an emergency operation to make, he comes as fast as he could, and meets the little boy's father who faced an accident and needs surgery. The father is furious, *"How can you arrive so late when my son is dying at the table there? Don't you have any ethics?"* The doctor assures him that he will do his best and to pray to god that the child becomes well soon! After the surgery, the doctor hurriedly goes away saying *"Any questions, ask the caregiver"* the boy's father is stunned. He wonders how the doctor can be so arrogant. He *sees* arrogance in the doctor and feels so. The caregiver tells the boy's father that the man was in the funeral of his son. He left it to attend the boy's surgery, now he has to return so that the funeral process can be complete. Why couldn't the boy's father believe that there may be something really important for the doctor to hurry away like that? He couldn't see beyond the requirements of his own son. His mind was clouded with judgment that the doctor doesn't know medical ethics. Emotions overrule our ego at times, we cannot see beyond us. Everything rotates around us, and nothing can be more important than to what matters to our own self. To get rid of yourself obsessed ego, you have to think for the greater good. You have to see way beyond your eyes can capture, feel from the heart that has no eyes but senses feelings that have humane touch.

The biggest challenge here is to know that certain beliefs are beyond you and need an effort to understand and change. Practicing in some ways can help you get greater control of your thoughts, emotions, and beliefs.

- Notice your thoughts. What energy do they possess? If they possess negative energy, just stop the mind from focusing on them. Think something completely different. Don't entertain those thoughts. If you know those thoughts are harmful let go of them. Positive vibrations help in inducing positive outcome.

- Replace the negative thought with a positive one. Feel the power that you can influence your own life and decide the direction it is going.If not anything try practicing meditation for a few minutes, make your mind blank, concentrate on the powers of the almighty and seek direction.

- Think of new thoughts. Things you want to change, say you are feeling anger because someone abused you. Rather than having revengeful thoughts, think how to give him an appropriate answer to gain his trust back. What offended him? Was he lashing out because of his own problems? Or was it something you really did wrong that he acted that way? In the former you have no hand, but in the later you can bring change so that lives could be better. Be the change you want to see.

- Awareness at all times is very important because the mind can misguide you. Ask the same question to yourself from different point of views. What would you have done if you have been in their shoes? We think only about us and get hurt. This hurt is not physical, it's mental. Our self-esteem, ego gets hurt. Think above ego. Think about causes, other probable outcomes, and what you can change and offer that could be detrimental in your mental peace. If you are egoistic, think about bringing peace to your own self.

Culture plays an important role in one's belief system and hence while the system is being challenged it is important to keep in mind where its roots are. Our beliefs lie embedded in our culture and are transmitted ahead by it. There are certain values or core beliefs which can never be challenged and there are some, breaking whom you could get punished. Each culture may have its own means to reinforce their ideology and set of beliefs. It is automatically ensured. Wisdom endowed to each culture gets passed ahead in their own systematic way. Keeping cultural impact in changing systems becomes relevant as such. To change about one self is easy; to change the mindsets of a whole culture is difficult. A tribal leader may be egoistic about his culture and think it a punishable offence to marry outside his race. No matter what modernism, science, theories, and advancement you present to him he will not be convinced. His ego about his superior race will not allow inter race marriage and his people will follow it blindly. Education and knowledge is the only thing that can change such viewpoints in due course of time. It will not take months but years and generations to overcome such self-egoistic beliefs.

Any change is a challenge as any growth, yet if seen through, in all its sincerity and humility, may set path for a much fuller experiencing life. Belief system is our creation and something we created has a chance of alteration for better growth. Emotions and the positive affirmations can make the mind believe what we want it to and may be our biggest ally in changing our old held beliefs. Someone rightly said that we carry our enemy inside so rather being aware of enemies outside be alert to one inside and act to save yourself when need be.........a successful life is a belief away!!

Changing Personality Traits Due To Changing Belief System:

Grass is always greener on the other side. Immaterial from which side you see it!!! I would say that is a typical human behavior, would you not!! Yes, I can see the smile on your face. Why is it that, what we are never satisfies us? Poor wishes for being rich, rich wishes to sleep in peace like the poor. If there ever was an ideal personality type, the queue to achieve that may have been longer than the one to lay your hands on. According to JK Rowling .... leave alone an adult even a child somewhere along the line wishes for a personality type which he is far different from. This somewhere gives us the hope that outward personality can be altered since the inborn type cannot be changed but may have chances of being molded. They surely can be redefined. According to theories which describe the personality type, it is believed that the inborn can't be changed but traits can be introduced and included. A man may have experiences of domestic violence in his home. It may have been normal for his eyes to see it and even consider it to be normal. He himself can become an abusive partner in life, as his inborn traits govern him, however because he has faced violence he can promise never to see his wife in similar shoes as he saw his mother suffering. It's a life choice, he has to make. He can change his belief system about physical violence and change his personality. His ego may not be his importance then, but a greater good in domestic life his preference.

The environment has control over our behavioral traits in a manner that is sometimes changeable. We may despise playing golf but live in a neighborhood where there are many golf players. Just to fit in we can play golf, feel our ego change and getting pride in it. However, when we change your locality and find a football ground around, our inbuilt love for football comes back, and we feel there is no greater way your ego gets satisfied than this big ball going into the nets than that small ball going into the hole. Our personalities that come zipped up in our gene pool can be questioned to some extent but could not be challenged completely though!!! However, recognize it properly. If its negative personality trait its best to get yourself rid of it. Only your level of education and understanding will guide you into understanding and identifying the right from the wrong. Each individual should take the opportunity to mold their personality in ways which brings out the best in them and their lives.

Research shows that people have self-theories and ego issues which define them as – fixed type and malleable type. The first lot defines their type being ones that can have fixed traits with not too much of inclination to change. They are the ones dangerous to society. They think highly of themselves, would not admit that they can be wrong, and cause pain and suffering to others. Their ego is so high that they do not have the time and space to think about others. The other group specified themselves more open to accepting their traits as dynamic entities with option of changing or developing with inputs of efforts and education. The latter group emerged to be better suited in life dynamics with higher chances of bouncing back. With a more open-minded attitude they would fare much better when their belief systems are re aligning.

If the Ego Is So Bad Should It Be Destroyed Completely?

So far that we have read, that ego can be both positive and negative depending how you use them. We associate the word ego more with its negative sense and everywhere people speaks about destroying ego to gain mental peace and stability in life. Bible, scriptures and all holy books are full of advices how ego should be destroyed. However, think of it in a positive and constructive way. Say you think you are fat and you need to lose weight. Your ego has superior views about people who are slim. So in order to walk parallel to your ego, you will try your best to lose weight and be attractive to your eyes if not anyone else's. It actually doesn't matter whether you are black or white, fat or slim, short or tall or any such physical factors. What matters is the inner you, and how your mind perceives the world through your eyes. You will be you, whether you lose weight or not. If you feed the negative in you it will grow and bloom, if the positive is fed, heard, seen, encouraged, positivity will be reflected in your life.

Night and day both make a lovely pair. Without each other they will not be beautiful in their own ways. Don't label yourself egoistic if you have certain negative traits. Transform them into positive. Transform yourself from ego centric to life centric. You cannot trample away the roses as they are in your path. Stop, smell, and admire its beauty. If everything is life centric, you appreciate the goodness in others, understand their situations and come to logical conclusions. You will be much more sensible to lives around you. Use your ego healthily, take up challenges, don't let your ego get hurt; show them what you are capable about. Nothing is as bad as going down in your own eyes. If you do, then only it matters. Increase competition, use ego to constructively analyze your faults and rectify them. It can be a benevolent force for greater good. Ego gives us a false sense of superior feeling. Use this feeling to be what you aspire to become. If slowly your ego centric feelings bring positive changes, it will also get transmitted in the society. Ultimately it will be for the greater good!!!

CHAPTER 4: THE ENERGY BEHIND OUR THOUGHTS

Whatever we visualize and experience around us is created by thoughts. Effectively all things physical around us are products of thoughts arising in minds, around the world. The science of matter says that matter is made of atoms and the energy of these atoms is derived from our conscious mind. This proves that the mind's energy is sent out as thoughts and that thoughts have energy leanings behind them. Thoughts could be positive or negative as a person could perceive. The power of thought is phenomenal and can be a life changer for any human being if driven or functioning towards right direction. Like it is said we are what we think. What we think consciously or unconsciously creates our life experiences and in turns our destiny. Maybe if we knew what damage a single negative thought could create, maybe we would run miles from even trying to do it. This power is generally not very rationally accepted that our reality is in our hands and the power to create is also in our minds. If this were clearly understood we would ascend beyond our physical self to one seeking spiritual existence too; hence the hesitation of humans to fully acknowledge the power of thought and its related energy.

Energy and Thought Dynamics:

It would be quite an eye opener to just visualize a normal day. Just remember the thought you got up with and how your day ahead went. We would realize that if we woke up and somehow the first thought in your mind seemed *"What a great morning! I think my project will wind up on time. Well, two more slides to go and we are ready to go."* The thought may cross your mind and you may even not remember it one hour from then. Yet a momentum has been provided to your day, a positive one at that and if at all you consciously assess the day at the end you may come to conclusion that the positive thought with its positive intent attracted most likely positive thoughts and that's how your day went. That precise is the energy behind a thought and its tendency to attract similar ones.

Another situation where John wakes up to a thought that he got up late for the day, since his alarm did not go on at the right time. He begins the day with annoyance that now he may be late for the meeting scheduled for the day, right in the morning. He may then face the consequences for the same from his team leader .His day almost goes as he predicts and the day ends up in a miserable note. Starting on a negative note may as well be the war lost at hand, because your mind decides so and vice versa!! Thoughts have energy. Negative thoughts create negative events and positive thoughts create positive events and outcome. Thoughts of your mind interact with the universe and whatever you think will attract only similar ones. They will bind with positive thoughts found in universe if you have been thinking positive and vice versa. Thinking you can do will result in you being able to do and achieve your goal and thinking you can't will ensure that you are unable to do it. Hence you should work towards creating a field of positive energy and have abundance of it.

The poem by Norman Van Horne brings out the cosmic equation between the thought and its power.

When you are gifted with the power of thought

It is a wonderful thing in a way,

But it can also create problem

If your thoughts tend to go astray.

The power of thought brings things to light

That we tend to postpone

But now folks with the power of thoughts,

Have today become quite known

So if you posses the power of thought

And don't know how to use it

Consult others who have the same quality

but very seldom abuse it.

For the Lord gave us the power of thought

To do with as we chose

So hang on to it, always

It is one power you don't want to lose!

Lot of us go through our lives being able to accomplish our goals and reaching success. Yet there are many who are unable to do it. Some are stuck in the vicious cycle of their mind thinking they can't do certain things. This may be on the basis that at some point in life they could not and hence they can't now or someone told them they can't and they believed them and ingrained that thought as a rule. So who is wrong here and where does the power to change it lie? For both the answer is the mind which thought so; hence the mind can be regulated in its thinking and made to think positive. As long as you believe and truly engage with the thought in your mind and your complete being, with a positive intent you have no fear of accomplishing something you have decided to!!! Negative or mind limiting thought can really bring you down in your life, it would be hence better to avoid company of people who are pessimists. Optimist will still try to instill a positive note even in the biggest of difficulties you may face.

As we discussed earlier, our thoughts are affected by our environment as much as our own belief system. So when it is realized over a period of time that a person 's belief system has become self limiting or self-defeating, there is a need to change. It is your habit of thought that drives your actions and not your desires. Lot of our beliefs function at the sub conscious level. Hence, we may feel lots of actions are automated because they just happen. Well, they happen because they come directed as a decision of your belief system. Result may or may not be desirable. This becomes clear that we set goals which are done consciously by us. Yet we are unable to reach them because the actions by the subconscious do not work towards the same.

How do we bring about the change in the pattern? We believe we can and then take actions towards the same. We give positive affirmations and surround ourselves with people who do the same and start the journey. We begin by changing the internal conditions first and then deal with ones outside.

Human Energies:

We have energy all around us. All matter around us works with energy behind them and as such humans also have an energy field around us. It may be difficult to point out and measure the energy field around us, yet specialized studies have shown that we are manifestations of energy ourselves. The fusion of our thoughts, emotions, intentions and the beliefs we hold forms our energy field and this interacts with the energies around to experience our life. Our body and the energy field around us have to be in sync to maintain balance. In case there is an imbalance of energies it shows as imbalances in the body too.

Human beings are made of the same things as the numerous things existing in the universe. Our basic existence depends on energy and so does the universe; we are hence all linked together in a loop .An intangible world, since it exists at the sub conscious level effects our tangible one or the physical one. Since this exists in conscious level. Our body hence is a projection of our energy field through our consciousness and our thoughts. This equilibrium can be disturbed by unbalanced thoughts and emotions. They also include our limiting beliefs we hold. If we realize that the power to change our energy field is inside us we are then with a power in our hand which is limitless.

From the beginning of the human kind it has been found that positive reactions and related energies dominate more than the negative ones. The Universe is considered a ball of energy which is reinventing itself by renewing old energy into new. Whatever goes out of these moves around and comes back into the original source. By consciously promoting our thoughts towards positive direction, we enable positive new energy released into our thoughts and action from the universal source making positive actions in our lives and helping our energy field to remain positive. With the law of attraction of universe, it will then attract more of positive and work for our well-being.

I have seen the brightest of minds falling down in agony due to the failure mind created. Like they say- it's all in the mind. Whichever way you take it. One the other end of spectrum I have seen people, pretty regular normal humans rise like a phoenix out of huge tragedies with their mind control and thoughts. Jean, a mother of two girls was on her way to her work place. A car accident on route to her work due to the other driver speeding left her paralyzed below waist. When she came out of hospital at the end of 3 months stay, barely able to move even in a wheel chair, life almost seemed over for her. She was one who always believed in living and not mere existing. With a severe phase of depression almost ruling her life, physical being too taking the beating of a weak mind almost lived difficult to live through. Just one sentence from her younger daughter, a 10-year-old who adored her super mom, who could always do everything…" *Mommy u love long drives, shall we go for one*". Michael, her spouse took it in his stride, moved her into their land rover beside him .The girls in tow the family went for a 3 hour long drive with no destination and returned home with wind still feeling through their hair. That night Jean felt life breathing back to her. One year down the line she did learn to navigate her wheel chair to the car, drives herself to work and s racing her car for championships. She won few, she won her life back.

Negative Thoughts Can Destroy You:

An untended mind can bring you down before anyone outside even attempts it. Rather lot of issues arising today in lives of people is due to negative outcomes of future events in their own minds which paralyze them much before the events even take place. Lot of times when you are ruminating through negative thoughts you may feel lost in woods. The feeling is sometimes scary and unnerving.

A mind filled with negative thoughts can & slowly will finish you as a person!! It is a matter of time when and how it occurs. When you see things in your life not turning out the way you thought they would, they usually have a way of bringing you confidence down. The faith in your own self wavers. And when you are feeling run down, we sometimes take decisions or make choices which go against your life. This further worsens the scenario, sometimes making people take extreme steps in their own lives before any intervention could take place.

When negative thoughts take root n your mind they can spread only branches and leaves of the same!! This negative pattern of thinking slowly permeates to your subconscious mind and your inner power responds to same frequencies. Like weeds it slowly and gradually dominates the fertile terrain of your mind, convincing it to move more towards negative than positive? This increases your worry; you then start to doubt your own selves and your capability! How then do we overcome this negative cycle and the doubt effect in our lives?

The Doubt Effect in Life:

The biggest reasons for a lot of setbacks in our lives are due to an aspect called doubt. Few things we do not realize are inter connected like fear, worry, apprehensions and so on. What we do not realize is that when we indulge in these it creates doubt in your mind!! With doubt enters failure and unpleasant experiences in life. The simple reason is you are what you think. So, if at all you give the mind a reason of self-doubt it starts believing in it. The actions we take are determined by thoughts. Hence if our thoughts are biased negatively so will our actions be.

Our beliefs create our reality. Sometimes when some contradicting or conflicting beliefs exist in us it creates obstacles in the creation of our reality. This then leads to sabotaging our own life goals. The moment you start thinking about why a certain thing is let's take, your project approval for the year, not working out you yourself set in a course of worry and doubt. All your energies which need to focus on what you are aiming at rather get distributed or channelized elsewhere. They go into focusing on negatives than you aim. The culprit is the doubt in your own thought process which will now move towards failure or non-attainment than a success. By unnecessary thinking and doubting your own capability you are pushing the goal away from you than attracting it with positive thinking. The thought energy and its manifestations are very relevant to be understood because they decide your reality by deciding your actions and behaviors.

It is surprising to come across a young child, may be a toddler, to say' *I can't draw*'!! '*It is difficult to sing a rhyme*". It comes naturally to them to do what they are asked to do immaterial of what the effective result may be. The drawing may have clouds in an ocean or the singing of rhyme may have all wrong lines but yet it is executed with all confidence and sincerity. Why as we grow this trait gets over shadowed with doubts. Self-doubt which does not surface in childhood raises its ugly head later on and tends to grow if you do not control it. One of the main reasons of failure in life is self-doubt!!we all have voices in our head telling us something or the other all the time. Some tell us good things about ourselves and some may tell you that you are not good enough for the world or not good enough to do a job. Over a period of time when you keep listening to same voices you start to internalize those views, right or wrong is another question altogether. This is when we become slower and less motivated to follow our dreams because we feel we may not reach there anyway. If these feelings from inside make a comfortable home in you that you are not worth enough they slowly eat away the peace of your mind and life and end up consuming you in the process. These then Lead to many problems like anxiety and depression to name a few and also manifesting itself as physical ailments like chronic back pain, weight loss or gain and so on.

It has been found that a lot of times this judgment of self destroys our important relationships as important as your marriage. They say when you begin a relationship on doubt, sooner or later it will succumb to it. Very few may be able to stand the test of self-doubt on relationships. Doubt can destroy many spheres of lives and one of them could be your marriage too. Understanding the example of Sheryl who was ending her 2 year old marriage because it suddenly felt that her husband was not the same anymore!!She had married James after a courtship of 3 years, blissfully happy in the same. It was this feeling in the relationship that made them take it to next level. She was euphoric that in James she had found her soul mate of life.

When they were to marry, 2 years back Sheryl not only developed cold feet she thoroughly started doubting whether it was the right step for her? Would James be the same when they were married? In spite of being an attractive woman she began doubting herself worth? Was she good enough for the successful entrepreneur and the list became endless!! Though they married over coming these shaky feelings, the relationship began on a doubtful note.

As the 1st year completed, their relation took a turn for worst. Sheryl began doubting and fabricating on all actions of her husband. Whether it was coming home late or just not being unable to answer her call. She insinuated thoughts of an affair she supposed he was having. She suddenly felt trapped, misunderstood and un-loved in the marriage. He too went into defensive lashing out at her at all junctures. Slowly their marriage started the walk on path of doom and they reached the state of filing for divorce. Why did this happen? How could this have been avoided? Was there a way?

Breaking Barriers and Healing Self:

It is natural to understand from what we discussed earlier that until all the negativity or the negative cross examining in the relationship is eliminated, there may not be any break through at all. Lot of times we struggle with issues of doubt, self-beliefs and fear in our lives. Sometimes it overwhelms us and sometimes we do overcome it!! How do we clean the slate of our mind of all the doubts that arise in our mind to reach our goal? Since doubt itself is a deep seated negative thought and we let it get nourishment by providing it more from our minds. We need to move out of this vicious cycle and stop playing to it! No one can get you out of it until you decide to do so. Yes, it is that simple.

"We can feed our faith with the Word, rather than feeding doubt with the devil's lies."

These simplified words in the Bible bring out the simple reality of life that it's on you and what you focus that your destiny depends on. Just as we exercise to grow our muscles stronger, so can we with our mind or our brain. Brain has the infinite capability of growing, as you shall train it. Mind has a habit of going into a comfortable space, even if that space is not what you intended to be in. It is scientifically proven that if the brain is stimulated in a certain way, it reacts in a certain manner. If your thoughts are of a certain frequency it initiates the mind to react and grow differently than it would have done with another set of thoughts. Hence it is linked that by controlling our thoughts and the energy behind them we can train our mind to behave in certain manner. The more we challenge our mind the more it reacts to stand up to your problems and helps find solutions.

Each human being is endowed with equal creative powers. How strange it is to visualize that having the same power in you each individual reaches different levels of success. If the power of human consciousness could be harnessed to maximum, we may be baffled by its power. Our consciousness exists as energy in the Universe. Our thoughts contain energy which interacts with the outer world and then lets us experience our life realities. Here the Universe does not initiate anything but merely facilitates the interaction of our thoughts & their energy. It is not concerned what you may experience as an outcome of energy exchange of thoughts in the Electromagnetic Universe. Effectively we decide what we shall experience through choosing our thoughts. If we consciously avoid negative thoughts in our circuit then we shall not attract the same from the outer world.

Intentions & Changing Reality:

What is an intention? It is a mental state that represents a commitment to carrying out an action in future. As we discussed before if we have a positive and productive intention and focus on it with all our concentration, it will initiate an action which will bring our reality as we dreamt it. That's how we change the existing reality. An idea precedes the reality, hence let the idea be the reality we want. To not be stuck in the cycle of what is not happening let us channelize our energies on what we want. It takes a while to even adjust to your own new pattern of thinking. We become so programmed to think in a certain way that the change puts you at discomfort and uneasiness. Hence, we may just summarize the steps as follows:

- Be aware of your thoughts and listen to what they say
- Consciously avoid negative thoughts and review the list of thoughts

- Picture or visualize what you see as your reality and imprint it as your intention
- Focus on that reality with undivided attention
- Send positive vibrations for the same in the Universe -   See the intention as your reality

In this process we realize that if we want something bad enough it somehow comes to you. With as simple a thing as securing an A grade, by a student who feels it is beyond him will need to have a complete mind set change before he begins with the thought of intending to do so. Not only does he start to believe that he can but he needs to put his focus on it. The concentration towards achieving the same has to be clubbed with the action supplementing the same. This journey starts the healing of self too beyond the ability to manifest the best possible outcome of your intention.

The body has been blessed with a self-repair mechanism. Whenever the mind stress gets discharged as stress to the body it can take the fight and flight response as you tell your mind to do. So, when we decide to break our cycle of thought and begin a new chain we ourselves become the co-creator of our healing. Everything starts from a thought and the thought produces or creates an action. So, if we have the control over our thoughts and mind we can control the physical manifestation of it and create a new reality. The reality may amaze us too. We may feel the need of a professional to activate our awareness but the power is within us to create our reality.

We have been blessed to have taken birth as a human on this earth. It is important to understand it is our birthright and privilege to express, feel, emote and love. Let's do it with compassion to ourselves and others around us. Life may be much more rewarding than you could have ever imagined. We choose our life, our choices are like our fingerprints, they make us what we are, so choose well, to live well.

CHAPTER 5: THE POWER OF PERCEPTION

Let's suppose it's been years you have left school and one fine day you bump into your school mate. Both of you gave each other good competition as far as grades and co-curricular activities were concerned. When the present scenario sinks in you realize that there now exists a vast difference. He is much more accomplished than you have been able to. Where does the difference lie? You realize after he explains that he has learned to overcome limiting thoughts and perceptions and risen in life by not calculating the score board and paying more attention to his actions. He changed his reality by going after his dreams and realizing them. Sometimes you see a mediocre grade achiever go on to make a success of their lives and some super achievers vanishing into oblivion. Why do we get stuck? May be the reason lies in our perception of life experiences and what we create out of it. The same experience may create different perceptions in different mind leading to different interpretations and outcomes. The perceptions of life, whether they are right or wrong, form the person you are in life!!! Are we caged in perceptions of past or is there a scope of reinventing it again?

What exactly is perception? Perception is a process by which individual organizes and understands their sensory images formed by their brain, to give meaning to things around them in their surroundings. In simple terms it just means how you see and become aware of things around you. They may be things and people who make your environment for the interactions of your life to occur. Perception is considered as one of the primary functions of your brain. The other is how your brain reacts to what you see, hear and feel around you. Your brain reacts to what you see, based on your previous experiences and interactions in life. These are in turn based on your core beliefs and thoughts. The process of perception is decided by internal and external factors, along with environmental and societal factors. The internal factors may include psychological factors that again are formed due to past experiences and social interactions with any particular event in life. This may indicate person's personality, his views towards life, and his behavior towards everyone and himself. The other internal factor is your learning from the environment you are raised up in. How people behaved to his success and failure, whether he was rebuked or patted for his achievements and basically the reactions that he received due to his actions. The external factors include the characteristics of stimuli, and its actions.

Perception from Neuro Linguistic Programming (NLP) Point Of View:

We experience life as a series of interactions, which may be independent of each other or linked. The scale of inputs to our mind is radically different in numbers than the actual experiences we go through. How do we experience things? How do we perceive our realty? One of the most important methods of understanding our reality and how we process information that is directed towards us is by a cognitive psychology model developed by Richard Bandler and John Grinder called Neuro Linguistic Programming (NLP). This works on the fundamental thought that Perception is Projection. Projection here means the way we see things. We build our own mental models with the help of our experiences and also the environment around us. We do it by decoding the experience and after understanding it put it away as a memory. We are continuously bombarded with information, in our waking hours through our senses. We may or may not have the need of all the information we are exposed to. How do we assimilate the information that we receive every day? We do it by taking in or absorbing only those information that stand out in our environment, that which seems logical and important to us, that which we find is linked to our past, its growth and development or may need the same in some source in future. The rest is lost. Because of the way our brain is wired, we generally adapt pattern recognition and reactions. Even when we perceive things, NLP, recognizes that we tend to filter things and most of our reality to reinforce what we already have assimilated in our lives or our beliefs.

NLP, talks about three inter related processes which make the process of perception happen.

Deletion- This is the process of leaving out or omitting pieces of information, which we tend to leave out either because we already know it. Or it creates conflict with what is already known to us. Here we pay selective attention to some information and overlooking some. A lot of this deleting occurs because of our survival mechanism which uses its discretion of what is good for your survival. The process of deletion not only happens in assimilating information it also expresses itself in our spoken and written word.

Distortion- This is looked upon as interpreting information in one's own mind following certain experiences and then storing it. It may be considered misrepresentation of reality or information. Just like deletion this might not be the perfect way of processing information or understanding it. What we see may not be true, similarly what we hear or feel may not project truth. But we still bring out a meaning to outside matters in a different way and store it in our brain.

Generalization- This is the process where we start drawing global conclusions or categorizing experiences based on a small set of experiences. For example, if a dear friend of ours lets us down by giving away a secret we shared, we go to the length of saying extreme sentences based on one or two interactions. *"Friends break our trust and we should not trust anyone."* This is oversimplifying the present fact beyond certain limits and drawing a biased conclusion. Generalizations in the long run form the base of our beliefs. This process may limit your way of analyzing anything; it may sometimes turn useful in some situations and harmful in some other situations. It is hence limiting in nature.

The three above mentioned processes are interlinked and all three works when we process information and perceive things around us.

The central principle of Gestalt's psychology is that *"The mind forms a global whole with self-organizing tendencies. When the human mind forms a percept, the whole has a reality of its own, independent of the parts "*. This may explain how certain things we perceive in a way are way beyond what they seem to be. Whoever said, what you see is not what it is, may have been intending to say precisely this. The reason why my reality is different than yours is simply because we have seen different things in life. No two persons can be in similar shoes. The things we perceive make us take our individual assumptions of that and react accordingly. We thus realize that by thinking what we do, feeling how we feel and behaving in a certain manner we have a hand in creating our reality. It is how we think and perceive creates our life situations and circumstances.

Let's take an example. Where are you right now? In your cubicle at work? Well, good. What are the things around you? You just made a quick glance of looking just now to see what is around you, at a place where you sit every day? Yes, u did have to and a lot of us would have done the same thing. Reason being that we never focus on certain things which are not as relevant as others! You never noticed the artificial flowers in the vase to be so real, till now. Sometimes we become so preoccupied with our lives we fail to notice a lot of things and rely on others perception of it to get by. We make an image of ourselves based on what others think of us, defying our true potentials.

"Whatever you hold in your mind will tend to occur in your life. If you continue to believe what you always thought of believing about yourself, you will continue to act the same way you have always acted. If you continue to act as you have always acted you will end up getting what you always got. If you want different results in your work or life, you have to change your perception of life. Change is always good if it's in the positive way, if it brings happiness, contentment and joy!" - Anonymous

Our Perception of Self:

How do we see ourselves in our own mind? That is how do we perceive ourselves? I would describe myself as a satisfied mother of two, a successful career person and an individual leading a practically fulfilling life with my immediate and extended family. A well-adjusted person in the society I live in. This is my description of myself, it is my idea of the kind of person I am. A part of it is my minds input; the rest is my perceptions about myself. That part which is beyond us has been assimilated subconsciously. Here you may question me, am I 100 percent accurate and correct? I may not be confident about the answer. I may be confident of some of my characteristics as a person but I may not know all my weaknesses and strengths, and it is very rarely possible!! As a human it is impossible to be so true to yourselves all the time in life that you evaluate yourself so honestly. Hence if we are not aware of everything about us, how is our self perception complete? And if it is not then how do we know where we have scope of improvement. I, as such then have to see how my perception co relates to my reality. Is it in sync with it or it is not. If it is not then comes the issue of facing a reality in our life which may not be completely true for us.

It may seem easy way out to agree that, what you are, is what your mind thinks you to be and you have no say in it. Can we say we are helpless due to our circumstances and hence cannot do anything about what we are? We may then never find our complete identity. It then gives you the leeway to get away with anything and have no accountability for it!! This is a scary probability, really!! What about our own efforts, our own deeds, actions, and responsibilities that can be taken to change our world? If we are not satisfied with our work, we have to look for another; you cannot afford to sit grumpy all day in office looking at the calendar just to get your pay check in time and live life unhappy. If you want change be the change, take the initiative, open the windows, breathe fresh air and work on lines of improvement, initiatives that you can take think of options, probabilities and attempts that can help you achieve what your core heart desires to. If you cannot get up from your seat you cannot walk ahead. You have to start somewhere to reach where you intend to. Give in your best, if it still doesn't happen, other factors may be involved, but trust me you will be much happier person to tell your own self that "I tried" and that makes all the difference.

If you are what they term you as a "housewife" and sometimes feel lost in household chores and changing nappies, and cooking meals, make a difference in your own life to see things turn positive in your way. Do some art and craft activities, join a gym and make that "Olalla" figure, learn a new language, attend a holistic life changing group meeting, read a book, open an online company specializing in things that you earned your degree about years back utilizing your talents, write a blog that vents out your feelings and emotions…in short do anything that makes you happy. Change your perception about yourself. If you keep the radar in others hand to make a difference in your life, it is not going to happen. You are solely responsible to take the first step to be happy. By being happy yourself you will also keep others happy around you, bring joy in others life and to the universe as a whole.

So to know your assets and to gain the best out of that we have, you have to accurately evaluate your self-perception and adjust it accordingly. This is not merely talking about self esteem or self worth; it is about recognizing you to reach what you deserve.

Others Perception of Me:

As humans we have a natural tendency of believing what others say of us. Perception and reality may hence not always coincide and collide into one. Sometimes we mislead ourselves by others perception of us, and lose our own selves. Other times we stand miles away from people's perception of us. How do we expect people to perceive us? Do we acknowledge the importance of their perception in our lives? We live in society and hence it is important give due respect to how people perceive us. We can't exist as islands, we share and co relate as individuals to see our life with respect to our environment.

How we see ourselves from our perspective may differ a lot from what others think of us, it may be similar in certain aspects but not all. Does this matter to us, yes it does!! Since how they think of us will decide how they behave, interact and communicate with us. This in turn decides the fate of our relationship, whether we see success or we account difference in opinion.

People's perception of us is based on our behavior towards them, towards our children, family, co-workers and society in general. Our change in behavior may change their perception of us. Depending on how we feel and rationalize our behavior changes. When we are satisfied and in relaxed state of mind we may almost be what others think us to be. What happens when we are under stress, do we still behave the same. The answer is no!! For example, Boris was considered as one of the most reliable and confident team members at work. As project deadline neared his behavior took on a strange turn. He would not only take impulsive decisions without consulting anyone, he started blaming others for his faults. He became nervy and aggressive from the confident and good natured team player. Is it not right that perception of people will change about him from what they held him to be?

For our relationships, for our career people's perception of us may decide its fate. So in your personal as well as professional lives, it plays a very important role. Hence if we pay more attention to our own behavior pattern and are able to understand our reactions, we may ease our journey of letting people perceive as we perceive ourselves. As we do this simultaneously we do need to be aware of the fact that people too may be wrong in our perception of us due to their reality. So it's important to believe your worth before questioning its reality and giving importance to what others think of us.

Perception and Self Esteem:

As humans it is but natural to have a sense of self-esteem. This is attributed to the identity we hold of ourselves. This self has evolved as an expression of experiences and interactions we have had in our life. It evolves over a period of time. It may have a positive leaning or negative leanings to it as a whole. When we look at our perception of self and others we arrive at an image we generally hold. Now this perception may not be always being right. Our experiences of our past experiences may have a way of distorting or clouding this image. Hence a compromised self-image or self-concept!!

For example, growing up in a family where bars of excellence were always high in all spheres, in spite of excelling in academics Rebecca was always pulled up for her physical appearance. She has always been addressed as 'skinny bones 'and 'scare crow' and this became a habit for her and somehow the imprints stayed in her mind forever. No matter how she evolved post puberty into an attractive teenager, she carried those labels subconsciously in her life. The external inputs from well wishers and friends could do nothing to change her opinion, leading her to form a compromised self-picture and a related low self-esteem. It's a harm that was done to her when internally she was growing as an individual. It's a scar that can only take years to overcome. She may become an attractive well-proportioned female in later years and get lots of admirers but in her heart of heart she will always feel sorry and sensitive, if someone ever called her 'thin'. Being thin is no longer a blessing for her unlike the millions of other girls who crave for it. She will always associate it with contempt as her self-esteem got questioned in her childhood again and again and it changed how she perceives herself as.

The self-concept has two attributes to it:

-<u>Self-esteem</u> – this is described as the opinion of self we have in our minds. This includes the regard towards our own self.

-<u>Self efficacy</u>- this could be described as level of competence or effectiveness of self towards achieving our goals.

Sometimes our distorted perception distorts our self image or self esteem. On other occasions if our self perception and self esteem is completely driven by contributions of others opinion then again, we are in big trouble!! We then need to take stock of ourselves. It is seen that people with low esteem are generally characterized by feelings of anxiety, unhappiness, inferiority complex and a general feeling of negativity. At the other end of spectrum are people with high self esteem. These people are generally found consistently responsible, highly committed to goals, confident yet working towards self betterment at any given point of time and opportunity.

Improving Self Esteem:

As our self esteem plays a very essential role in our lives and our behavior. It is pertinent to recognize that self esteem is rooted in our perceptions and directly affects it. There is a definite need to improve on self esteem if it falls lower than it should be. The pointers below may list out the broad areas to be worked on –

- <u>Avoid too much self criticism</u>
  We may have heard and carried labels for years together but to break the cycle it is important to not continue indulging in damaging self talk. This means consciously avoiding defeating input and giving positive ones instead.

- <u>Appreciate your strengths</u>
  We generally have a tendency to dwell in our drawbacks or flaws, putting complete focus on that. It is hence required of us to focus on our strengths, immaterial of how big or small they are. There is always and added advantage in life if we acknowledge our strengths and be happy about them.

- <u>Recognize and accept rejection positively</u>
  It is impossible for any person to be liked by all. If a person or a group does not appreciate your efforts and like you, it's ok. You are not born to please everybody. What matters most if your own self esteem and worth. Never compromise on self respect. If you fall down in your own eyes, you can never look up. Hold your head high, take all these rejections as experiences, and work on improving and changing things about you and around you that can make a difference.

It is relevant to accept self as we are, including our flaws. Until we realize that we are imperfect the journey towards perfection does not get started. As we work and improve our self esteem our perception and perspectives in life also show a change for better.

Perception Changes Biology:

Is it possible that by thinking how I do something, I can actually change the status of my health and my biological self? This feels more like a science fiction experiment and a little unbelievable at that!! But here is the truth, it really can and we have experimental evidence which proved it. Life hence gives you different ways of improving and changing the gift of life, if you wish to!! We have always believed that it was our gene pool which controlled how we turned out, but beside the genes controlling a lot of us it is the environment which controls how we turn out.

Let's see through the experiment we are talking about to understand it better. In 1982 stem cell biologist, Bruce Lipton trying to understand cells information processing system was cloning stem cells in Petri dish. He would put one cell in a Petri dish and wait for it to multiply; slowly he had a colony of cells. He divided the group into 3 different Petri dishes with 3 different bases or chemicals and waited again for them to divide. The result was stunning. The cells were cloned so they had to be genetically same but all three groups had different cells in them. This proved that environment controls cell behavior beside the DNA makeup it has.

This brings to us the understanding that cells are fundamental units of our existence and have the ability to change us through our environment and our thoughts. Just like cells change according to their environment our perception changes according to what is around us and what we think. If we think positive our perceptions are likely to be positive based and vice versa. Different feelings and perceptions have the capacity to make our mind work differently so it is important to keep a track of them. We have the power to create our life let us do it the right way.

Increased amount of stress strain tensions and negative influences in our life also create bad health to us. We suffer from depression, suicidal tendencies, migraine, insomnia, obesity, anxiety, and hyper sensitivity to others and their behaviors around us, even resorting to drugs and alcohol to get release. Everything is in our mind, these mental issues need to be changed, to be treated and sought necessary help to overcome, so as to see positive health benefits that we can have. What we think what we perceive and what we make out from a particular situation affects our mindset deeply and accordingly our heath. Sonia got rejected in love. She perceived herself as a failure, unwanted and unloved. She went into depression and started binge eating. Gained more than 20kilos and became what she thought of herself as, -- failure, unwanted and unloved. Had she taken a control of her situation, went out socially, meet new people, go on blind dates, start to work out being more attractive, and more interesting, she could have found her true mate and not done the destruction she brought upon herself.

Here the law of attraction again materializes. If you send strong vibrations to your mind by thinking positively your mental traits and in turn your neural activity forms new connections in mind and reacts in a positive mode and perceives things which make you feel that life is getting life goals closer to you. We can work towards increased awareness of selves to create a better biology and reality.

Trigger Thoughts- Miscommunication and Conflict:

In life come various circumstances where a situation may just derail you, even if momentarily. It may not be the situation itself but your understanding of it which leads you to feel the way you feel. Something linked to the situation in your memory triggers this feeling. It basically is your perception of the event which creates the havoc. Let's take the small example of a normal working day. Consider a small act of not being able to provide snack box to your child in the morning. How that makes you feel right in the morning, you start feeling worthless and pessimistic. Guilt crops up to make you feel you are not a good enough mother. Reality is you were unwell, woke up a little later than usual and realized there was not enough time to make anything. Or simply as usual your child refuses the food you gave her to eat and declares a hunger strike. This simple chain should not be putting you through so much of stress and agony, yet it does.

This could be defined as a trigger which makes you feel so. The fact that you could not provide food for your kid before leaving for school is a trigger. Your mind goes into an over drive and produces the worst image possible of that situation which may not be true. It builds up image of your child starving, becoming cranky not being able to express hunger and making tantrums at school and so on, which is far from truth. The child may have really not felt hungry or will compensate by eating the whole lunchbox later. This is the mind's automatic response or the habitual response which comes from past experiences. If this habitual response takes a negative stand then it may give rise to internal conflict. It may lead to miscommunication in certain cases. We may not realize it but our brain sometimes gets more burdened with negative thinking than positive, if u would like to believe. Many a times we also do not feel eating early morning and its okay to skip breakfast once in a while, it's the child's process also of learning, that once I miss food at this hour I will have to wait till I get the next break. Force feeding, yelling and causing stress, will not only hamper you physically but also strain your relationship with your child. She may end up puking or feeling unwell after that and choose to blame you for this outcome. There are thought traps the mind falls into and triggers a reaction. It is very important to hold control on this trigger as they may cloud your thinking and perception, both!!

Miscommunication: How common is it to come across a conversation like the one mentioned below, between a couple!!

-I asked you to pick up clothes from laundry.

- No, u did not...Rather you said you would!!

-Yes, I did. When you mentioned going to Laura's skating class I thought you would automatically do so.

- I thought you meant me to pick Laura

I thought, I hoped, I assumed- all these cause miscommunications and altered sense of perception. Communication among people depends on their ability to decode and respond to each other's mental model. If they are similar minded, the communication between them is more effective than if they are not. Problems in communication arise because of our subjective experiences than the external factors we blame them on. This word exchange above shows a complete mismatch between what was reality and what was perceived. Such miscommunications lead to conflict and further damage. Hence saying perception is reality may not always be true in all circumstances. You must verbally be explicit and share your concerns and matters with your partner in order to get peace at home. You cannot expect everyone to understand as no two people can be in same shoes. No two people think alike, so if you want miscommunication not to happen and ruin your day, communicate well and mind it hints do not work well always, be vocal and express positively.

Changing Self Perception For Better Outcome:

We have a lesser say in changing other people's perception of us. We have a bigger say in working on our perception of ourselves. This can be manipulated or worked on more for desirable results. We may in the process realize that lot of our own perceptions about ourselves are biased or sometimes wrong. They may hence create what are called misconceptions. They alter your understanding too. If we want to change few areas of our lives we have to first accept that it needs change. We may or may not become perfect but we make be a closer version of that. Since our self-perceptions create our reality and decide our behavior we may take our negative perceptions along with us and create a reality miles away from what we intended to be. How do we go about doing it? There are few steps which may help us in our endeavor:

- <u>Assess your own perception</u> –what is your picture you hold in mind of our own. What are the strengths and flaws? Can you accurately point them down? Make a list.

- <u>Collaborate with an external input</u>- when you cross check your opinion of yourself with another human being, your well wisher whom you can trust, you see your thoughts either being accepted as true or negated as false. This gives you a balanced view, outside you to compare with. Next time you sit with your friends do not play truth or dare, ask them to play a game with you where each one of you will list down five positive and five negative points about each others. You will be amazed at the outcome.

-     <u>Challenge yourself</u>-as you realize where the disharmony is in your perception, evaluate your situation as to how bad or good it is!! Then take steps to come out of your comfort area to rectify that.

-     <u>Imitate and internalize habits you want to learn</u>-Sometimes putting on a brave front really does make you feel brave!! Copying a habit which you want to internalize may be a beginning of it. Adopt anything that you look up to, or think that would make you coveted, respected and admired.

These vivid steps more or less may bring about the start of journey to shift in your perception. When we manage our perceptions, it comes in close tandem to our reality. Slowly the perception of reality fades and just the reality remains, which is a fact and certain.

It is within us to change the way how we see reality and experience it, it may be a bigger boon than being able to change the substance of reality. We hence need to keep working towards fine tuning our existing mind map in various ways to make our reality the best suited to us. It is not only important to realize that we have the power to change our present reality, it is equally important to work towards it with the right intention to reach our maximum potential laden within us. Within us resides the power to be the best copy we can of our image projected to the world, let us work towards making it worthwhile!!!

CHAPTER 6: THERE ARE NO COINCIDENCES…IT'S WHAT WE ATTRACT

"Cherish your visions. Cherish your ideals.

Cherish the music that stirs in your heart, the beauty that forms in your mind,

the loveliness that drapes your purest thoughts,

for out of them will grow all delightful conditions,

all heavenly environment- of these, if you but remain true to them,

your world will at last be built. "

- James Allen

Jennifer shares her birthday with her mom-in-law. Her father shares his birthday with her father-in-law. Could this be just a coincidence or a link of some learning!! We are all fascinated by coincidences. Are they by chance or is there something more meaningful beyond that. Each one of us would be interested in knowing about it. There are times when they happen in our life and we just move on, not letting it impact us. It is much later some reminder of it lets us know how it impacted us. We may as well begin the journey to understand that. When we start living our life filled with gratitude and appreciation of coincidences numerous possibilities open up.

Everyone who comes to our life or crosses our path has a role to play in our life. Someone may become so important that we might consider them our 'life'. But the fact remains, everyone even our parents, love, pets, come to our life to play a part, they are chapters in our lives that makes the whole story eventful and beautiful in some way or the other. Some of these encounters break our heart, make us sad yet they provide us with experience. Some of the chapters makes us happy and content and gives powerful parts in transforming our story. Everything depends on our choice. And nature has its own way of giving hints and providing options to us. It's time we recognize those and identify with them to change our life for the better. We just have to reach those secret messages, see with our eyes wide open. They say co incidence is god's way of remaining anonymous and stay connected to our fates. Everything has a hidden meaning, everything is predestined, and planned we just have to find out why and when and how, so that things that depresses us finds a way to look at the greener pastures and give our self a feel good factor. Don't step back thinking that something bad has happened to you, if it's denied to you it probably means there is something even better that awaits your way!

Manifesting Self:

As humans we are capable of harnessing thoughts, questioning, and asking about things that don't seem to be right in the first place. Our thoughts which are produced in our mind and beliefs we hold close to our heart, together form our reality. What we think and believe becomes our reality. So, we manifest what we think and perceive around us. We probably never recognize the power we hold or maybe we have been trained to behave so, as our conditioning. This process of manifesting is at work in our lives every moment, most of the times without our consciousness and realization. Each thought is linked to an energy flow or vibration within and around us. This energy attracts energy similar in nature, if I send out negative energy; it can only attract that as per The Law of attraction working in the Universe.

It is as such very essential that we comprehend the fact that how we perceive our world or our reality on the whole is how it will manifest itself for us. Almost like a mirror, reflecting back exactly what you showed it. Every thought that passes your mind counts, even the ones you did not notice!! What we assume is that thoughts that do not play an active role in our brains, those the bigger Universe would have surely not registered!! We are mistaken in thinking so. The Universe is always tuned to each one of us and responding or replying to us. The power of praying cannot be overlooked, as that in words tell the greater powers what we want and need, however the simple wishes that cross our heart everyday…" oh I wish I got that red dress", "OH I wish I get admitted to that University", these are equally echoed in the universe and have its own time and space to bestow it on you. It is we who are not tuned to this interaction that we fail to notice it. We need to awaken our consciousness and expand it to let it catch the energy vibrations which help us further on our way to our goals and desires.

Let us take the example of a growing teenager Timothy, who thinks "I am no good". Well, in all likelihood she will be no good and attract experiences in her life which will superimpose the same thought!! This will then form the foundation of her belief system and as she progresses in life will carry the same blue print making it her reality. She in the process of thinking that she cannot excel in studies, have not studied well, and thus failed miserably, in her manifestation of the thought that she will not look good in the red dress, missed out on looking good on the prom night and missed to dance with the cute boy in her neighborhood. Co incidences came her way with her books falling off the rack when she was busy finding her nail polish or making her catch the same path that had the cute red dress to indicate her to choose well, so that she achieves what her core most heart desires. Its nature's way of speaking that she ignored and become prey to her own destructive negative thought of being "no good" and reestablishing the fact.

Our thoughts and the related energy is the key foundation of creating our reality. The creation of our reality and understanding it has puzzled our minds since time immemorial. As mankind, we have been in pursuit of it for years and have found few logical pieces which fit in the frame. Our energies have been directed at finding our place in the larger universe we exist in and the interaction we have with it. The biggest game changer, as they call it, in this field is the emergence of Quantum Physics as a theory in the field. This theory explains our existence in the Universe beyond our physical world and also our experiences therein explaining our present reality. It emphasizes that we create our reality every moment through our mind thoughts which then influences the reality that is perceived as a combination of energy and awareness. Everything is co related, and we don't always understand them properly. But everything happens for a reason and has a rigid complex network of actions and reactions intertwined with every permutation and combination of choices we make.

The Energy Interactions in Universe:

Our world consists of a consistent interchange of vibrating waves of energy. As we think, the produced thought has energy associated with it. The law of energy states that the kind of thoughts and related energy we put out, similar is attracted to it. The whole Universe is made up of energy and hence energy just passes from one to another. We are connected to the Universe and vice versa. An indefinable world affects the definable world of our experiences. We are masters of our perceived world and slaves of the unperceived. Whatever we experience in this physical world we give credit to people and situations, but what we do not perceive, and lies in the greater powers of the Universe, we call it destiny fate or co incidences. Have you ever given it a thought that for something to hap[pen in one particular way in your life, so many lives, so many forces, so many fates, and so many choices are interlinked. It's actually a tough job to make everything fall in the right place, and therefore the nature's way of making you take a particular path of making a choice by hinting the correct direction through co incidences.

We have an associated electromagnetic field surrounding us. Our neurons create nerve impulses which are electric signals and as they are formed they create electric fields around our body and electromagnetic waves outside it which can travel from the body into the Universe. The nerve impulses create human electricity and create human electromagnetic fields. The human electromagnetic field can be felt and has capacity to influence people around us. For example, when we come close to certain people we start feeling more energetic and active. Yet there are people who make us feel depressed and drained when we near them. This explains the energy transfers occurring between the electromagnetic fields of people.

A changing magnetic field will induce a changing electric field and so on, as they are linked. This interaction creates electromagnetic waves which can travel beyond air, solid materials and reach space, surrounded by the ultimate Universe. The presence of these waves can also be shown through machines which can catch them and measure it. Hence, it's proved to be science. Our body electricity is an important concept we need to understand before we understand how it helps in manifesting itself. How does the universe communicate with itself and all its constituents? As we go about our daily chores we are not even aware of the huge information and energy exchange occurring within our mind, body and beyond with the Universal system. Waves from throughout the cosmic system move through and around the Earth and human bodies within. And we radiate the UV and higher energies accordingly as interchange occur. When we focus on a thing as our goal, our consciousness directs its energies towards it and sends high frequencies waves which then further attract similar energies from the universe to make that desire manifest itself. Similarly if we are unable to send out strong energies we may not be able to see the dreams being manifested. . The challenge is thus in being able to utilize our ever shifting perspective so that we can focus upon the thoughts that can make a positive difference. It is what we attract!!! And to make our perspectives in our goal we have to put all our energy in it. The Universe can only guide us in taking the right path with the help of co-incidences and self-talking into our minds.

Everything Happens For A Reason:

You are house hunting; each one you see is not exactly what you want. You are constantly vibing out thoughts about acquiring the right property into the Universe. There is an energy exchange and it's happening without your knowledge, through your thoughts, your actions and your desires. You are preoccupied and as you get into elevator to work, you bump into a person on his way too. He apologizes for almost banging into you. As you get talking you realize he deals in real estate.

Within next two days you are signing the deal for the house suited perfectly for your requirement.

Jane had been thinking of her roommate Alison, since the last two days after almost a month of their graduation, since she saw a movie in which the main protagonists name was Alison. She would eventually forget calling her. The same evening, she got a call from Alison about a new opening at a research institute, suited for her. Both the above experiences seem too good to be true, yet they are. Curiously, these unexpected events happening as they did would seem sheer coincidences. But believe it or not they were meant to happen. It is only when these occurrences happen more than random, do we notice or pay attention to them. The moment this noticing happens do we become aware that may be there is a reason behind them!!

In this Universe nothing happens by chance. There is no such thing as coincidences. In our lives when a coincidence happens we generally ignore it and move on, thinking it to be trivial. Do we ever try and look for a message in it? We don't even try to see the significance of the event. We tend to do this may be, because we have been conditioned to do so. All things around us are interconnected; the Universe is a mesh of energies. They are hidden because we can't see them; rather we are not tuned to catching them and hence fail to see their presence. This may be one of the most pinching realities of mankind. We were sent by God to achieve greatness in our lives and yet we are unable to see his guidance in the form of energies around us. We are born with divinity in us. As we grow it gets enveloped into layers of ignorance, ego, indifference and absence of unconditional love for mankind. This feeling holds us in achieving what we were intended to, when we can and should do. Our intuition which we are blessed with gets more and more dormant as we move in life because we never took any initiative to let it blossom!! The conditioning of our mind and environment lets it lie below layers of ignorance and abandonment.

Are we not hampering our own growth by doing the same? Why do we always seem to move with an agenda in life? Why is it that the mind functions at a level of being one tracked into believing that life has to always give you only meaningful experiences? If not the interaction is not worthwhile. The need of the hour is to open your own self to more flexibility with experiences, thoughts and intuitions you are blessed with. You need to realize that if you keep your heart and soul open to experiences and are ready to go through them without any agenda in mind, they will be more fruitful in our learning. We are so open to advices from people around us, almost getting brainwashed by their beliefs, but do not pay any attention to nature's way of speaking or getting connected to us. We ignore co incidences, as random actions, and also override our gut feelings to what the society tells us to do. Is it so hard to concentrate what the Universe tells us to do through its various tools? It is one of the ways to let positive energies flow towards you without hindrance and let the law of attraction work with more effectiveness. So, if you suddenly realize your life being intervened with coincidences of sorts, finding strange links and dreams and actions that point out a specific thing or event in your life, do not overlook, think of it as a message from beyond. Be open to them, you need not necessarily keep waiting for them to channelize your life, just become aware. These are energies around you to assist you further in your way towards your desires and their manifestation. Do not sit idle looking for hints, remember god helps them those who helps themselves, get up on your feet, start walking, and once you do you will be amazed by the road signs that god will leave on your way to reach your goal.

Influencing Your Own Energy Force:

As our universe, the matters around us too are made up of vibrating particles of different frequencies. We as human beings too correspond to a certain wave frequency, which changes depending on how we are feeling or how and what we emote!! Yes, this is true. How I feel is defined by what I think. As I think so shall I feel and so shall I attract!! Simple, isn't it? When we feel a certain emotion, positive or negative, we are left feeling a certain way. We vibrate at certain frequencies in tune with that feeling, when the feeling changes so do the vibrations change. So, effectively we are the Co-creator of our reality by being able to get manifestations according to our desires. We are the Co-creator of god's intentions on earth and beyond. We are the architects of our own fortunes; we just have to identify the ways in which the superior forces connect to us. Good is always balanced with bad. If you are having bumpy rides, stay focused, concentrate your goals, and connect with your inner self so that the whole Universe conspires in fulfilling your dreams. If not give you what you want, it will give you experience to conquer greater. Never say "I want a car", say it like this "make me capable enough so that I earn so much that I am able to buy a car for myself" that shows gratitude to the higher powers and if you give respect you receive the same yourself. Law of attraction remember?

There are certain key points that we need to register in mind when we consciously want this law to function in our lives to enable manifesting our desired realities.

> **Hold the right thought**: this means that providing the right attitude and thinking for manifestations to occur. Feel the right feel and hold the right thoughts. Confused? Don't be! It means building bridging thoughts between where we are and where we want to be. There should not be too much discrepancy between the thought we hold and where we are. Because where we want to be will be reached in small steps from where we are.

The cushion time: there is a certain time lapse between what you intend on your subject and that being manifested. So, go with the flow and let it happen. Enjoy the experiences on the faith, they teach you something and knowledge is always necessary for growth. The more we feel a certain reality is possible the sooner it will manifest. The lesser the resistance, i.e., having doubts of difficulty in reaching it, the easier your pathway. Our long-held beliefs sometimes create obstacles in turning certain aspects in reality, and sometimes environment acts as hindrance. These are all tests to prove your passion. So, be ready and hold patience as your desired experiences open out for you.

- **Believe in the process**: when you want certain thought to be manifest as your reality, you have to learn to let go of your feeling to have that as a result. Work on problem solving approach than a solution seeking one. Learn to trust the process and flow with it holding all positivity. Let impatience not tempt

you, but you reinforce on your mind with the right vibrations of achieving and abundance than absence and scarcity. Time frame will work itself out perfectly.

Synchronicity:

This concept was described by the Swiss psychologist **Carl Jung**. His description of the concept is as follows,

"The conceptual relationship of minds, defined as the relationship between ideas, is intricately structured in its own logical way and gives rise to relationships that are not casual in nature. These relationships can manifest themselves as simultaneous occurrences that are meaningfully related. "

Our realization that we are all interconnected, in the vast Universe may bring to fore a lot of happenings of our lives whose understanding isn't in our realm. Just like a computer network connects numerous of them through its system, we humans too are connected or networked to the universe. As if it's a giant operating system with complex software that controls and manifests the life of many around us in almost co incidental way to cross paths and share the fortunes. Our human limitations sometimes stop up from understanding a lot of interaction in the bigger picture.

Say you dreamt of a particular person all of a sudden and that person gives you a call after months without any reason, just to say "hi". This explains that any or every event is beyond just a random coincidence. Each one of us has experienced random thoughts in our minds and suddenly one particular day we see them manifesting as a reality in front of us. During my pregnancy one fine day I craved for cheese sticks. My husband was not around so I couldn't go out all alone and buy them. Evening my neighbor comes home just to visit me with a box full of cheese sticks! Sheer co incidence? Or some unfathomable powers interplay? How as a person should you take that? As we develop our intuition we become more aware of our environment. This in turn makes the connection between our conscious and sub-conscious mind stronger. We start following our instincts more and give a chance to the dormant lying divinity to connect with our physical reality. This is where our brain with its evolved automated system which edits a lot without our knowledge starts to fall in synch in synchronization with the outer world. We have the power to influence our environment. We have the choice to be more connected to oneself.

Each day of our life we experience meaningful coincidences and synchronicities which we attract through our energy. Once we start believing in them we shall realize that they hold a lot of importance since they could be the life altering omen or messages for our lives. The Synchronicities and omens in our lives sometimes don't make sense in the middle of journey. We are just expected to follow that inner feeling and voice telling you to follow your intuition. If you stop inner resistance to this happening, to the coincidences and signs in your life, your purpose and destiny will come into your clear view. Lot of random pieces suddenly clicks into an art form created for you!!! At the right moment it shall reveal to you in its entirety. It is then we realize that we were just being directed all the while.   So be aware and pursue them to their positive conclusion.

Principles of Manifesting:

As we become more open to experience the events as they unfold in our lives with a more open attitude, with unconditional love towards fellow beings and gratitude and appreciation to our Creator, we become more aware at conscious level too. We learn to be in the moment and enjoy it. This itself puts our focus in that particular moment and makes us emit higher energy frequencies. Coincidences, synchronicities and messages from beyond are how the Universe arranges for the manifestation of our reality. It just needs to be focused and have the right intent, and as an automated reaction the Universe starts aligning it to our reality. As we move towards this process of manifesting we need to remember few basic principles which have to be followed religiously to reach your destination.

- **Principle one: let go of limiting beliefs**
  "I CAN'T" was a limiting belief Andrea held since childhood. It not only made her have low energy negative thoughts, those also became her reality. I can't make friends made her stay aloof and lonely. She became a series of such living realities. To begin with manifesting in a person like her it became evidently clear that that she had to clear her vibration loop. For this the step is to ask for guidance from the Universe to let go of the belief. She for sure would also endure lot of negative experiences and feelings that would try to prove her belief. Yet these are her learning towards her ultimate goal. With practice, spontaneously behaving in manner that helps her naturally eliminate procrastination and get rid of mental obsessions. To have the unshakable trust that as these limiting beliefs fall of, a cleaner

space will have positive thoughts and reactions more. She would start to believe in her own power.

- **Principle two : have clarity**

We have to necessarily have clear intentions in mind for them to manifest. Rebecca, a mother of two and a teacher at school had such an overtly emotional mindset that she found it difficult to concentrate on a single intent. Her emotional upheaval created clutter for thoughts. So how does she clear the slate of her mind? If there are any doubts or conflicts in mind they surely stand as obstacles in your way. We need to deal with them to progress forward. This could be done by either visualization or making a list for your own clarity. If doing it in mind seems impossible make a list on a piece of paper and stick it on a place you can see every day and make little changes in yourself to achieve it daily. A vibrant picture lets you have a positive feel and an optimistic environment.

- **Principle three: think, believe & achieve**

The process of manifesting is more of us connecting back to our own inherent divinity and greatness as human soul. Once you decide on your subject of manifesting, you have to spend time with it. It's about getting comfortable with the fact that I would like this in my life and this is possible. Work towards that goal, trust your intuition and belief follow the divine interventions for it manifests itself in many ways, and it will happen. Let your expectations in life be real, they should not be absurd. They should not be hindrances to your path of bigger goal. Expectations should never equal to greed. For that is like burning fire insatiable.

- **Principle four: have faith**

Once you have decided to place your trust in the process, do not be impatient or anxious. It does not matter where you stand today, how bad your situation is or how horrible the prospects of your future feel like, just move with faith and love in your heart. It may feel you are walking in a certain direction out of blind faith but that is not what it is. You will receive guidance always through those little voices in your head that tell you to do exactly what is to be done, and co incidences and synchronicities will be on your way. You have to just let it happen, do not hasten any feeling and keep your expectations at bay. Stay calm and overcome the anxiety of outcome.

- **Principle five: the helping hand**

As you slowly inch towards seeing your manifestation turning into reality through the process, know that you help in the process is increasing your awareness level. You have to know that energies around will match up with the intention you set out for yourself. Start feeling happiness around you than expecting things to happen. When you realize you are happy because you feel it from within, you will realize that the manifestation is only a byproduct not the end result. Your happiness and peace matter more.

The potential for all our realities lies here waiting to be accessed. They wait for us to connect. Like said before, we unfortunately have lost our connections to this field due to conditioning of our mind and our ego which stands strong between us and our reality. It succeeds only when we are able to learn to maintain a dynamic and interactive relationship of our life energy and the energies of the world. It is something that we become, not something we create. This as we have now understood is not as simple as it sounds. The process of manifestation completely relics on the right balance and tuning of our thoughts, beliefs, environmental and social influences, and the list goes on. Even if one of them is out of line, you will feel it difficult to hit the nail on the head. It is not just about positive and wishful thinking it is about your psyche aligning with your outer world.

Towards A More Awakened Being:

Who would not want to be more effective, who wouldn't want to become happier and more satisfied in living the game of life? What does it feel like if you are able to do so with your heightened awareness levels? Beyond happiness, if there was something like that!!! As you become more aware you are awakened beyond your realization. It may be a little curious life to you as it happens, but it is a matter of getting used to. It may take a while to imbibe that we are in a different space than others because in the broader sense you have just found how to be you. Lot of things matter to you differently and may change their status in your life. Does that mean you go into a state of no inertia and movement? No, it means you realize the truth of your being. This acquired knowledge does not send ripples in your mind. Rather it settles you into a peaceful and stable state.

You are less in disagreement with others. You may feel lesser need to change others when any disagreement occurs. This feels like the beginning of the wholeness we have been striving towards all our lives. In spite of being alone you are not lonely!! You feel connected and continue your life on self decided pace though in tandem with the external world. It does not take you away from your existing physical world. It just teaches you to effectively live the same life with a much better understanding of occurrences and life goals. Here we also need to remember that what we have reached is just a different level of awareness or the principle, the individual potential. The journey of this principle converting to the manifestations remains. We have to start believing in our creator power for them to happen; he will not come to everyone and have a heart to heart talk. He will manifest himself through his various ways to communicating that we call as 'voices in the head', intuition, co incidence, and fate destiny and so on. We have to keep our eyes open so as to see. If we close and shut ourselves from experiencing the true potentials that life holds and plans for us, we will lose our chance to excel. We anyways lose a lot by comparing our self with others. The only one worth comparable is the one which is us a day before. We have to see that we have made a progress everyday towards reaching our goal. We are what we attract, and by vibing the positivity from us we will also attract positivity in our lives.

CHAPTER 7: LUCK, KARMA…..A CYCLE OF CAUSE AND EFFECT

We all have a lucky charm…a pendant, a pen, an exam board, a favorite set of clothing, a particular color -very few can deny this fact. We take them to our important exam, our important meetings where things of importance occur and also have it with us when we feel we need an extra push, beyond what is in our hand. How often we scream in sheer excitement when we win a lucky draw or an unexpected lottery!!! What good luck? Isn't it? Our happiness overflows when we meet such situations when we get something out of the blue and unexpected, and something of real good worth. It could be winning a trip abroad… winning a new product for home, and so on. How exactly do we describe luck? The dictionary meaning terms it as, *"any success or failure apparently brought by chance rather than through one's effort or own actions."* For example, in a match when the first throw results in a basket, everyone applauds *"what good luck"*. Now whether it was sheer skill or was it chance it is debatable! Some people always consider themselves lucky and some people feel they always have a run of bad luck. Why is it like that? Does something called luck, fate or karma really exist?

On the other hand, let us consider this; our work is not shaping up as we would expect it to with all hard work we are putting in. Or suddenly one day you are faced with a vacation notice of your apartment, the money you had saved and put in shares loses value and you make a loss…. a series of such misfortunes start piling up. The moment anything bad happens we rush to find reasons on which we could put the blame on. We all somehow strive to prove that we are not at fault. Then who is it that we can play the blame game with? And immediately it comes out of your own mind that you are a victim of fate or this was destined, it's all in His hands. What are we to do? Sometimes life situations overcome you with their sheer unexpectedness and sudden life changing pattern that you are left wondering, what actually happened? And you conveniently put it fate.

We expect life to run in a certain manner, sometimes it does and it makes us happy. Yet again sometimes just does not go according to our wishes and it makes us all stressed. Life does not conform to our expectations always. Things do not always happen as per our convenience and comfort, and that's how life is supposed to be! And yet we end up asking ourselves, why me? Why not someone else? Who actually controls our destiny? Who is in charge? Does it not surprise us that if all was actually in His hands the world today would have been a perfect place for all of us to live? It may have had the best of circumstances we could have ever imagined. If God was the creator of our destinies how could there have been so many discrepancies in destiny of millions of people around us? Imagine you had the power to write the fate of your child, as a parent what would you do? Well, naturally you would put down the best of education, health and wealth attributes and a seemingly perfect future as the power is in your hand as a parent, would you not?? Then how do we imagine that HE as our creator could put to our destiny all the hardships and challenges we face in our lives? Even if it were the worst of our enemies we were to wish upon certain things we would not wish for the disastrous situations that happen in some lives around us. What explains these things? It shows that it is not all fate and destiny. There are things beyond luck which anyway is a random feature in life. What exactly is it? Well, it is karma? Buddhists and Hindus believe that it is **Karma** or the 'Law of Cause & Effect' that can lead one to salvation. The way you give yourself to the rest of the world through your deeds will eventually come back to you. Karma is a direct reflection of our actions and deeds we have been indulging in this life. It could also be described as our psychic energy which projects from us as our actions. Karma works on its own independent time frame and hence it cannot be as such predicted.

The Law of Karma or Law of Cause & Effect:

The law of Karma states that each individual destiny is decided by their own karma or actions and not by good or bad luck as people say. Rather good luck is a manifestation of good deeds, either of present life or the lives you have lived before. We walk hand in hand with our karma as we lead our life, making our own choices and facing their consequences of same. Karma and destiny have a very direct and close relationship with each other. Destiny is the accumulated result of our karma. We have lived our lives listening to the age-old wisdom *"As you sow, so shall you reap"*. That clearly shows that our destiny is in our control, since we are the masters of our action and the choices behind them. Being more or less lucky than others is a matter of understanding that it is directly linked to your karma. So, in simple terms it is not fate or luck, it is your karma knocking at your doors. Good or bad is all what you have done. You will sometimes see that actions taken long time ago will spring up results in the present and will continue in future as the ripple continues.

The law of cause and effect is also sometimes called the law of ultimate justice. This law transcends time and space. It may be this reason when encountered with it in strange ways we are at loss to understand it. When we see a young man in his prime years losing his life in a car accident, without even with a chance of saving him we wonder how the law makes logic in such circumstances, leaving us hurting and angry. Since our understanding of the law is limited and we are co-relating it to only the current period and time, it happens beyond us. We are unable to even see any learning from the same when such incidents happen. Like said before this law moves beyond time and space, the law may sometimes take years before a wrong deed of someone somewhere is set right. But it will be done and there is no escape. Time, location or area has no impact on it because it does not work on the physical bodies we are carrying around. Even though this law states that every deed is rewarded and good begets good. Bad begets bad. In spite of such clear workings of it the ultimate aim is not to punish anyone. It works more as an enforcing agent in our lives for our learning to happen. It is more as a teaching for mankind to keep the balance of universe. Nobody knows when the law will impact us for which karma of life so it does good to ask the almighty's grace every moment we live.

This law functions on Newton's Third Law of Motion that any action has equal and opposite reaction. Any action performed by us produces equal and opposite reaction, either at the same time or a different time frame. This law is a universal principle which governs all living beings. It not only controls but decides our destiny, through our good or bad deeds. When we evaluate our life and realize that certain things are not the way it should be and wonder that in spite of our actions being right, why is it that we face hardships and challenges. The answer may lie in our own being, understanding it may take a while. What we are evaluating is where we see ourselves right now at the present moment. Do we know how our karmic account is and where we stand today, may be not because we account for ourselves now not knowing how we have fared before. Karmic accounts carry on just like our souls from one life to another. The debts and credits keep changing as do our deeds. As if there is a cosmic accountant who keeps an account of everyone's good and bad deeds in present and previous lives and twists and turns the fate of individuals accordingly. The cosmos or the universe as if maintains a record, immaterial of our life a balance is strived upon as far as karma goes. This may come as a piece of good news to us because then control on your destiny comes back to your own hands. This was initially invested in hands, beyond our control, to Him. Well, he does control our destiny but not in creating it but in guiding us every way towards it by giving us the courage and strength to make and live our choices.

This law is a basic spiritual principle which is a common thread in all religions whether it is Christianity, Buddhism, Hinduism, Is and so many others too. This brings to fore the knowledge that each religion may look different and may feel different in living it yet works towards the common goal of brotherhood and compassion towards all. The Holy Bible also brings to fore the same thought in these chosen words *"as ye sow, so also shall you reap"*. It clearly brings out that you reap what you yourself have sown, good or bad as you chose. Hence you stand responsible for the same, for your actions, and deeds towards this world and humanity at large. As you created it, you shall not shy away from experiencing its effects too. If you engage in good deeds be assured you shall meet the same in return. It stands true for bad deeds too. Everything we stand for today is the sum total of all our actions executed till that particular point of time. If at all we see a lot of things going haywire in our life, we need to redirect our actions to fix them. By doing that we help ourselves in changing the direction of our lives. Hence there is no such thing as accident, chance or luck …it is what your actions have been and what you got in return. The actions are the cause and the situations are the effect we are faced with. What we have been, are today and will be tomorrow is in turn creating the conditions and situations of our life and helping build our future in front of us. As we react to all that is around we will decide how our future transforms accordingly. This law not only gives us the understanding of our experiences and reality, it also provides us with a tool to improve the same for better. When we acknowledge that the power is within us to bring about the change in what we call as fate or destiny we feel all powerful and our consciousness relates to it and works towards it. Rather than feeling miserable and transferring the blame on something or someone it is time we took responsibility for our reality and also for changing it if we are not satisfied and happy about it.

Karmic Account:

In life we may have come across situations when we are in a social gathering we meet a completely new group of people. Over the evening two instances occur. In one instance you meet person A and distinctly take a dislike to him, for no visible reason. You get a feeling that you can't be friends, not even good acquaintances and are not even keen on any further interactions. There is no explanation, yet your feelings are strong. In the next instance you meet person B and take an instant liking to her or rather spend the evening with her. You seem to have a lot in common. There is no explanation, yet there is a strong connect.

What explains this?? The hidden answer for both situations lies in the law of karma.

It is explained by the concept of karmic account. A karmic account is an account between two souls and their interlinked karmas. Almost like a bank balance sheet, with its credits and debits. This is where the similarity ends because in your bank account net balance involves interactions or cancelling between credits and debits. But in karmic account your credits or karma is in one group and bad karma or debit in another. Both are never mixed to give your final karmic account. So every soul faces the consequence of his bad and good karma separately y and till these accounts between the two souls are settled they keep taking birth into a new life. Our identity may be as that of a person but our life exists on interactions with others. In our existence we deal with others and hence create accounts of debit and credit with them. We are now living connections which we made in our past life and are currently dealing with the related accounts. The emotions we feel towards another person are based on these karmic accounts or the energy exchange between the two souls. When the karmic account of a soul is zero, he is liberated and becomes a divine human being.

How do we manage these accounts? They say happiness and good karma always complement each other and it is something that we create. If we tone down our expectations a bit, tend to be a little more compassionate and forgiving in our relationships and honest to our own feelings without any pretense, we will be more at peace with ourselves. If these particular thoughts are internalized and executed in all situations under any circumstances then we have reached a different awareness level than otherwise. This state leads to inner peace and induces a state of bliss. Being in such state can only produce good karma and good thoughts, which will then fuel back happiness. The cycle goes on.

Changing Your Luck with Changing Of Karma:

The first step to changing karma is to understand that it directly affects our destiny and if anything related to it has to change it has to be the seed of karma that is the thought. If we are to change it we have to begin with changing our mindset and regulating our thoughts. Lot of times we hold so many doubts in our mind that they make us mentally vulnerable. Doubts in personal life, professional life, and social life create clutters, and clutters are negative. They bring the negative vibes out of us. To have a clutter free mind is difficult proposition, and so it is difficult to monitor thoughts as it needs a lot of alertness of mind. That itself may be a huge goal to achieve. There is a simpler way, to monitor how you feel. The link is simple; if you are happy or possess positive thoughts your mind sends positive energies to the universe. As you send out such vibrations the more it will attract of similar kind as per the law of attraction. Nobody has ever been poor by giving, give the best to the rest of the world, and good karma will follow your steps back home.

If you reflect you will see that whenever things go wrong or don't go our way we feel let down, stressed and low in energy. The thoughts sent in this state are going to be low vibration weak thoughts, and also will attract similar forming a chain of negatively charged thoughts. It is very easy to fall prey to the thought that we are victims of luck. But with the right awareness and effort when it does occur to you that the reason for everything lays within you, you sit back to see changes in your life.

Imagine a man being held as a captive for days, he was tortured every day and prayed for his faith to be restored. When his captors were caught and he was released, the man was asked what his most dreadful experience was ever. He said that once he was almost about to give up on faith and losing my compassion on my captors. People were taken aback by his response, and then he explained. He said by torturing him every day the captors were increasing their bad karma and cleansing his negative karma. They were inviting future negative incidents on themselves, and he instead was getting closer to good karma and enlightenment. He felt himself as the decider of their misfortunes and this gave him all the energy he required to sustain. It's amazing isn't it? Maybe it's too good to be true or applied in our everyday life? But we can of course try to let go of the negatives, turn them into positives, and look for the good everything holds. Everything that's denied or comes as a negative set back has some underlying meaning or hidden blessing in some form or the other. Holding on to this belief and working towards making life of yours and others around you will generate good karma, and automatically good luck. You can create your own good luck when you change your karma, how you deal with a situation, how you respond to the challenges in life, how you fight and give in your best to bring the best of what is offered to you. When your mindset is changed your actions change, when your actions change your karma change, when your karma changes good luck automatically follows you.

To move towards our goal there are certain thoughts we need to be aware of-

-**work towards positive frame**: This would mean consciously thinking positive thoughts. As the law of attraction works every moment in the universe around us we should be hence aware of what we think. Lot of our long-held beliefs, behavior and experiences also put obstacles in this pathway.

-**aware of limiting system**: many a times in life we face a set back because we are so tuned to a certain belief system we don't want to be flexible at all. For example, a student thinking that saving can happen only when we hold a job. If we practically think saving is a mindset and it can be done even while a student is in college and yet holding an evening job. It may just be a limiting belief since that is what the person has grown up with. Learning to be fluid and have the patience to go with the flow is essential.

-**positive language**: if we notice we generally have a tendency to start sentences with don't, can't and so on. It may be a minor reflection yet goes a long way in furthering your goal of changing your thoughts. Instead of using language which brings down your energy level it is better to rephrase your sentence with a positive note. Rather than saying *"Don't break the glass while going to keep in the sink"* it serves a better purpose to say" *keep the glass carefully"*. Language and words is a very important tool, in making your karma have a positive influence. It may be always better to adopt a positive mindset and keep moving. Dwelling over past mistakes and worrying over them does not serve any purpose. Creating good karma is need of the hour.

- **controlling our responses**: life does not allow us to control our external circumstances. But we are always in a position to decide how we react to it. Responding is always in our hand and that has to be done responsibly. You need to have good intent at heart. Keeping god's grace while we use our mind to make our choices and decisions always helps. You seem to have a universal support rallying for you.

- **keep good lifestyle**: a life which has no discipline with regard to food, sleep, exercise, work and related issues always tends to be stressed. A cluttered mind always gives skewed decisions. It is of importance then that we eat and sleep right. No excess of any kind or deprivation of any should bring about imbalances in mind which are then reflected in your thoughts and actions.

-**manage ego**: we think no end of ourselves and we always seem to be in an illusion that we are right and can never go wrong. Whatever wrong happens to us we try to find a person or luck to blame for our misfortunes. Instead of saying *"I was unlucky"* say" I *will try better next time"*; you know you can. Egoistical thinking bothers how we act or react. So to maintain a balance between 'me' and its right manifestation is our responsibility.

Meditation:

How can we make new karma? Being mindful is one way to go about it. By being unmindful of our own thoughts we get imprisoned and stuck in our cultivated lifetime habits of not seeing and observing but just reacting and blaming. If we have to change our karma we have to bring about a change in all this. We have to see clearly to be able to do all this. The most important journey a human can make in this world is the one within. The journey where you get to know the real you. Finding peace within you can see appreciate and accept life as it comes rather than wanting things be your way. Meditation helps us in increasing our awareness and also to help us begin our journey within. As human beings we have potential not known to us, yet latent within us. How do we connect to that potential?

Meditation is one of the most widely accepted and practiced technique which is used to modify the habit patterns of the mind as does speaking or retraining to speak in certain ways. But like any other skill it needs learning and practice to achieve the desired results. When we are mindful of our own existence and thoughts and just sit doing nothing, somehow the impulses that keep arising now and then, related to certain thoughts just fade away. Few destructive thoughts also pass away into background. Hence the process to changing karma begins with changing our own mind.

The mind is the instrument which produces all our thoughts, feelings and helps us experience and perceive our reality. So, when we control the outward activity of mind and try to still our mind by practice we decide to break the flow of old karma and create new and positive karma right then. When we are not engaged in anything and stop just to watch the moments in their entirety, our understanding and clarity of them increases. In this way we start creating better moments for our future by investing in present act dedicated to that. We create our own fate or luck by practicing inner peace, as whenever life throws lemons at us we should make lemonade out of it isn't it?

Let's take an example to understand this. If Adam is a person in whom traits like kindness and being non-judgmental were dominant in his previous life. In his present life he has been blessed with negative traits of being short tempered and jealous in nature. By not strengthening the kindness and not being biased traits of his previous life, they will fade away and not show up in the next life. They become weak with no practice. Whereas if Adam realizes that to overcome his anger and biased attitude of now he could start meditating and start developing the positive traits from before by his choice, they become strong and manifest again in the next life. If he is able to consciously feel these things during meditating then sooner or later they will manifest in normal occurrences and also when the situations are under stress. This not only increases your awareness but also controls chances of you creating bad karma anymore because you will be able to exercise control in adverse situations. He will be in better control of his feelings, behavior actions and hence his responses to a particular event will also be softened. If he gives out positivity from himself, positivity will be attracted to him and good luck will follow him wherever he goes.

Nothing ever goes away even if we wish it to. Any karma good or bad comes around to you and you should be prepared. If you have indulged in bad deeds they will come back to teach you what you ought to, so sometimes bad karma is a help in disguise since it goes to teach you a particular lesson. Maybe this is why it explains that we have ups and downs in life, every good has a bad to follow in some step or other later. We need to focus and strengthen ourselves to embrace each other equally and convert the negatives with our positives. Love can win the bitterest of heart, compassion can make one go miles. We ultimately are directed to living our life in such a manner that doing so we are able to not only assist each other but also enrich them and us in the process. It should never ever be in our mind to hold a negative intention for anyone or ever try to harm them intentionally. For it will come back to us in some form be in this life or next, but it will. When this becomes our internal belief system we will be at peace with our existence and learn to appreciate the goodness that life has to offer to us.

Grace and Gratitude:

How frequently do we use sentences like these, *"By God's grace my house was built in record time and could move in right when I retired"?\ "Adele could manage the scholarship for college by God's grace and continue higher education". "By god's grace we are blessed with baby girl this time"* What do we actually mean when we say these statements? Every living and nonliving presence in and around us in universe is God's creation. We are defined by His presence and not vice versa, this is what we try to mean when we use those words and most of us firmly believe in them. Can it then be possible that we can ever neglect His presence, sincerely never. As children of God we need to live and act constantly under His guidance. He always plants hint in our way to help us make our choices. We sometimes call it as premonition, déjàvu, co-incidence, dream, divine intervention etc. Cherishing His presence amongst us, we need to follow His doctrine to lead meaningful lives. How do we define grace? In dictionary terms it means, *'God's unmerited favor'.* This is what we believe. We feel we all know what it means and stutter when asked to explain. We feel this is His goodwill, kindness and a favor to his children who may or may not deserve it. We keep doing our good or bad karma, not understanding what outcome it will bring, and blame luck or god for our misfortunes… so many times we cry and say *"Why god why me?"* we seldom look into our own actions, think that we had choices to live our life differently yet we choose to what led us now., our lives are intertwined, our fates are connected, our karmas jointly influence our present situation if two people are involved in an incident. Humanity should be the only religion that god would have loved us to follow, yet we blame others, fight, wish bad luck, encourage destructive thoughts and create self-imposed chaos on our life. All our actions are not justified and we knowingly or unknowingly indulge in bad deeds and yet we are given His mercy and shown the way to our best destination. Here it is of importance that we must be in position to accept His grace. We must have the understanding that we have to make the use of what he has endowed us with and reach our intended destiny. We should be aware that this grace has opportunities for our deliverance and release from our sins. It is with this understanding we follow the path of changing our karma.

Feeling grateful for this grace, goes a long way as an acknowledgement to Him for all we have received. When our being is filled with gratitude for all we have, for our fellow beings that travel the path of life with us and for all resources, natural and otherwise, we may just be overwhelmed! It may then instill in us the courage and power from within to change our karmic cycle to reach our destiny. It may be a reawaking of its kind.

CHAPTER 8: DETERMINING YOUR FUTURE THROUGH FAITH

"Have faith, things will get better"

"Faith can move mountains"

"Let your faith be stronger than your fear"

How often do we use statements like these, whenever we see someone in challenging situations and trying to stay afloat?? What do you think we believe in when words as these springs out of our mind? It is the concept called faith which forms the foundation of such belief. I have faith that my pre-school kid has a good and patient teacher. A mother has faith that her son will get a good job. Can anyone prove by reason that these holds true, no. Yet we hold the belief. Who instills such feelings in us? How do we define faith? As we see it, it's a belief, confidence or trust in a person, object, religion, idea etc. despite the absence of proof and scientific reasoning. It then has to be something that is unique in which we invest our complete confidence without having any knowledge of proof. Faith arises from the fact that there is someone beyond our human level, Our Creator, who holds us all together and has our best interest in mind. Sometimes we wonder about our relationship with Him! How does he reveal Himself to us. We assume that being our creator He has prepared a extremely glorious future filled with happiness. This forms the foundation of our trust in him and his powers that he exercises in this world through us. Everyone sends here has some duty or work to do, and we simply believe that while doing so, we have to have faith in our powers and His guidance. It can be compared to a parent and child relationship, where the whole nurturing process is as similar. As the child has faith in parent just by the virtue of being a parent, it is the same with human and god relationship. All are of equal worth in His eyes and there are no favorites amongst them. It is by our own deeds that we invite his blessing or wrath to what we call as misfortune or boon in this world. None receive any special favors from Him, and neither any special consideration. Like we discussed in the first chapter the strength the faith the trust has to be there on our own powers. "I am" capable of doing what I intend to do. The faith has to be there on the powers inside. He does not bestow some with supernatural powers and create the rest ordinary. It's upon us whether we utilize our capabilities to 100% or not that makes it all the different.

Our life experiences and all things that happen to us seem to happen in a pre-decided manner. Meanwhile it is also true that life means what we make of it or the meaning we give to it. This duality exists in the world and both are true. Our existence and the universe are mutually linked, and hence our destiny is also linked. Somewhere the God's intent for us and our own actions towards it have to align, for us to experience satisfaction in life. So, there are few parts of our life that are alterable and some are not.

There is something then which stands as obstacle between God's will and our reality. Why is there a discrepancy between the two? That is because His will has to be translated into actions by us. Our karma or deeds sometime move us away from our destined future. It's rightly said that we build our own future. It's in our hands! How do we go about changing it for the better? We begin by first understanding our present and move consciously towards determining our goals. When we find ourselves at a juncture, where we feel that the direction that our life is taking is not what we imagine for ourselves, it is time to take stock. If you look back at past too often you do not find the present interesting. If you look at the future all the time, you are not putting enough efforts in the present. To make life perfect you have to work on it every second that you are experiencing it. That is now!

There are situations in life where we find we are pushed to the wall for no reason at all, it's time to hold your faith and take a review of it. Introspecting about it may reveal that the present situation is a creation of your own karma and its manifestation. Hence each person can develop self-awareness, self acceptance through interactions with others and to one's own self and bring about a change in the same. We were created to manifest our realities in the infinite Universe. There is an invisible thread that joins us to God. Yet it does not mean that we can just wait for our life be navigated by him. We may hold strong belief of god but should we let our latent potential go waste which we have been granted by birth. All our life we have heard this *"god helps them those who help themselves"* how true is that! Our endeavor as such should be to utilize the same for our own betterment. The thing to remember here is that while we move towards finding our true self it should be with the awareness of faith. We must have trust in the cosmic powers and our own capabilities to bring about any change in our lives. We live in a timeless situation. Claim something it is already yours, it already exists in the mind of infinity in the depth of your potentials, in the efforts that you can put in.

Time is an illusion of our senses; human mind is the greatest time machine. We keep swinging from our memories, of what happened and try to make images in our brain of what our future could be. In the midst of it all we neglect the present. We should have faith in the fact that whatever happened in the past has given us some lesson or experiences to fall back on as cushioning our strengths. We should have faith in our future that everything will be well, by being optimistic and trusting the almighty powers to do good to us. But most importantly we should have faith in our strengths to day to make the changes necessary for a timeless satisfaction in our souls on the day we die that we did everything we could in our hands. We just didn't lie back and let time flow away and waste our potentials. We are what we think our self to be, we have the power to do that, when we simply pass the present and it becomes our past we simply become the omnipotent "I am" our self.

How do we create a future which we deem fit for ourselves? How is it that two people with more or less similar resources, start at same beginning point yet reach different destination? We as humans have the basic human neurology at birth. Our ability to execute anything in life is based on how well we control our nervous energy or the workings of mind. It could be as basic as cooking your breakfast or as challenging as being a NASA scientist, it all depends on the control of your thoughts and mind. The more effectively we harness this energy the better we are in our ventures of life. NLP works on these thoughts and teaches finer understandings of them.

Its basic principle states that we see and experience world through our senses and then translate the sensory input to thought process, both at conscious and unconscious levels. These thoughts then trigger the neurological system into action. These actions are then represented as your emotions, behavior and feelings. It also explains how our language and words we use to speak directly influence our experience of any happening or event. The last aspect of NLP deals with the programming of the person or the internal map of a person. Whatever we see or are based on our internal map which means our patterns of thinking, our beliefs and faith and individual decision making strategies. Hence the NLP theory helps in strategizing your learning from life also to have the best possible outcome. NLP could be described as a manual for your brain distinctly developed for you to help you in determining your future. The origin of this theory is also rooted in how the founders of theory where amazed at how some people could have the mettle to beat all odds and still succeed. And certain other people who have everything at yet turn out as failures. There are many around us who drift through life with no real purpose and no desire and passion. Such people can never succeed no matter how much faith they have in the almighty!

Destiny Fallacy

"Success and failure are not overnight experiences. It's the small decisions along the way that cause people to fail or succeed ". – Anthony Robbins

"My fate is in his hands". "Fate turned against me". "We eventually came to terms with our fate ". Listening to such words one would feel that these are the most helpless beings on earth, but it is not so. It is the attitude we adopt towards our fate or destiny. Destiny seems an external factor but it is not. The link to it's working lie inside us. It is the subconscious mind which actually controls the action of mind more than the conscious part in enacting part. It's a faith in our abilities and beliefs that compel one to personally stand up and shape our future.

We have come to believe that our lives are not completely under our control and yet again they are not so much controlled by other factors that we have no way of intervening in them. They say our destiny is shaped by how we have made our life choices and by our karma influence. Faith is a factor which helps us hold positive thoughts and work towards making our future better. Destiny is often understood as the" route that life takes". Our karma is one of the factors which influence it. We sometimes use the word fate and destiny in interchangeable terms yet they are different. Fate seems more fatalistic and predetermined in nature as also understood by examples we started with. Destiny on the other hand appears to have more optimistic feel to it since it feels there is human hand in shaping it. We make our own future by the thoughts we think and the actions we take based on them.

Have Faith in The Words That Come Out of You, As They Shape Your Future:

What comes out of one's mouth as words goes into someone's ears impacting them with positive or negative energy. The languages we use to communicate with others are basically the thoughts working inside our heads. These thoughts initiate action which on continuous repetition becomes habits. The habits describe us or our character. We are known to others by our habitual behavior or our character. *"He is a great guy"*, *"She is an amazing mom, all full of energy"*," *she is so rude and impatient"*, *"he is very diplomatic and untrustworthy"*; these traits describe the person's character in a way. People have gathered these feelings about us by interacting with us on a regular basis. While interacting with us they have been pleased with the words that have come out of our mouths that must and should have contained something positive in order to nurture such feelings about us. So how the relation will be with men around us depends on our words that we use to express ourselves. While you should have faith in yourself to achieve your dreams you should also have faith in the words as they shape your future and your environment that eventually helps in helping you grow positively as a person. You cannot say anything to anyone and later feel apologetic, trust me it will never be the same again. These thoughts and the actions repeated over a period of time become our identity. If thoughts are positive the outcome is generally positive and the resulting actions will be uplifting in nature. On holding them at regular basis we move our self towards a better future scope. When you think of a thought and visualize it getting a success out of it, the subconscious mind supports it in every way possible. It is better to be not under the common illusion held by people that we are helpless as far as our future is concerned. Than remaining in our present state we can always move towards a better one and create it ourselves.

God and The Concept of Faith. - In Him or In Us?

What do we understand when we speak of god? What is God to you? Do you know God? Most people would say that god is someone omnipotent and omnipresent everywhere, not bound with the shackles of religion, guiding and protecting us, shaping our lives as we live. He is superior force that guides our life. What do you mean by a superior force? When you term something as 'Superior' alternatively you term or consider yourself as inferior consciously and subconsciously, which again hinders and restricts yourself, your growth and creative abilities. You always look for appreciation and approval for someone else apart from you or a sign from god that you did the right thing. Neurolinguistic thinkers differ from ordinary thinkers by what they say is, whatever super power you consider as external, is deeply inherent and rooted in you, and you are the sole owner and creator and generator of that power what you call God. so, as I think- "*God is the superimposed creation of faith in the infinite human minds*", which they might like to place on anything, it can be a relationship, an ideal, your country, your children...anything that you would like to hold back to for living life.

This faith gives you intellectual and emotional security, as well all are floating in this vast space, like tiny particles. Our mind is also a vast limitless ocean of space, and unless we hold on to something or have faith in something, we would get lost. In other words, lose our minds, logical, reasonable minds having the higher order brain driving our thoughts and actions and rather tend to get driven by our reptilian brain. We live in a timeless situation is equivalent to living in a vast ocean of time and space, where your or my life occupies a very miniscule amount of it, which can be termed as negligible. Say an average of 60-70 years is nothing in this vast universe of time and space. So living in this huge timeless ness of space and life, what you personally imagine and think about your life, you can turn it into realty for the time being in which you exist. Time is limited for everybody. You just have a few years to make a change in your life or society as a whole. What our mind imagines or thinks that becomes a reality for us, and we have faith in that. Our thoughts and actions are driven by that imagination, and consciously or unconsciously/subconsciously we keep doing things that take us closer to that reality perceived in our mind. All of us have a huge potential subconscious mind hidden within, which creates our destiny as it works like a machine, listening to the directives of our creative thinking and imaginations. Like an ice berg, a tip only shows. So, whatever you think, you claim that or find that happening in reality, because you thought about it, you wanted it and you created it. So, we should be careful of our thoughts that evade our mind. No negative entrants there. Only positive ones are to be entertained. Have faith in them and turn them into reality.

Mind The Creator Of Our Destiny:

Mind is the most powerful tool in helping create our destiny. How each person uses it differentiates where each one will stand. Mind is blessed with infinite powers and is capable of achieving almost everything it desires. The issue of present times is that a very few people actually know what powers lie in them and how to go about using them and most importantly few have faith in them. So, when the question of creating or determining your future comes to fore, mind is the most integral part in the whole process. We belong to this universe, as a part of it. And everything here is made of energy. Our thoughts too are forms of energy which have related frequencies and vibrations. When we look at it from the point of view of law of attraction, it clearly specifies that energy always attracts alike, which means of similar nature. The thoughts hence sent out which are of high vibrations and positive in nature will attract only those and vice versa. It is as such important to be always aware that we function in an attraction-based universe. Every dynamic in it are then working on the same principle.

Though we believe completely in the proverb *"Man proposes God disposes"*, it is equally true that man has the onus of free will. This dichotomy exists and is completely true. We have the freedom to make our choices and this goes a long way in proving true a lot of leaders with humble origins, who had faith that they could and they did so. The character of a person is determined by the traits he has learned which themselves are habits of mind. Evolving characters can always be changed by changing deeds of karma behind them as we learn to mold our destiny we begin so with the thoughts of our mind. Sometime this freedom of free will gets overwritten by some irrational beliefs and poor judgment and thinking on our behalf. This situation should then be overcome with new understanding, faith and utilize the power of our own mind to turn our dreams come true. Take the example of Walt Disney, who was fired by a newspaper editor because he "*lacked imagination and had no good ideas*" He had faith in his pencil and what he made out of his life in the times that he lived and much way beyond that till this day is history! You will be surprised by many success stories like these where people did not care about what others told them about what they are, had faith in their abilities and succeeded in life.

Destiny plays an important role in how our life shapes up. Life is a mixture of what destiny stores for us and how much we walk up to it with our own efforts to see what is in store. Sometimes it feels that in spite of our perseverance things do not click when we expect them to. They rather click when we least expect them to. Nothing in life culminates before its due time or also if it is not meant for us. We choose the path we would like to walk on, then why at the smallest of slights do we put the blame on either destiny or others around us? The freedom of free will come with the instruction of taking responsibility when need be and not the careless attitude of resting error on someone else's shoulders. Stop the blame game, start acting!

How Stereotype Thoughts Disrupt Our Faith and Abilities:

As human beings we sow a thought and it results in thinking. The thought creates an action, the action creates a habit, the habit creates traits and that in turn creates your character and destiny. Ultimately we are the creator of our destiny. Power of changing it also lies within us. Imagine a routine week day. You wake to your alarm, get off the bed from same side, walk to your bathroom and brush in the same way as yesterday, have a shower using the same soap, come out and groom yourselves as you always do, eat the same breakfast and meet the same people at work, return home with same car pool people, feel the same emotions as any other day and wind up the day. So, you lived another day just like the previous one. No new changes and no new redefining.

What did we do differently than yesterday, well nothing? After following such routine year after year, the brain also gets stuck in a pattern of thinking firing same neurons day after day. When each day we repeat our thoughts, feelings and emotions then how can we expect the mind to present a new line of thought. If our mind thinks continually upon a chain of thought, a channel is formed into which this thought force runs automatically as a habit. When such a habit of thought is practiced all life it also survives of passing of the physical body and gets carried over into the next life as a thought predisposition and ability. It becomes the standard way of how thinking would happen in the new life too. Our faith in doing something better, differently and to stand out gets disrupted, and we fall prey to flowing time and flow with the tide rather navigating through it.

We earlier saw how mind always has a mental image of a thought that is how it interprets it for itself. All these images get accumulated in the present life and form the basis of the next life. When we do our karma it simultaneously affects two ways —one is the mind which made the body indulge in the action or karma, the other being the people around you who are influenced by it. So, every moment when the karma is influencing the mind and the people in your interaction sphere, at the same time you are creating situations and interactions of your future life. Whether you are conscious about it or not are another matter but it is automatically happening. Every thought is a part of the cause and effect chain, every karma has a past thought influencing it and the same karma influencing your own future at the same time.

Desire- Thought-Action-Destiny

The thought and action chain have to be changed for any new beginning. If in another instance we wake up one day and decide to do things differently, our brain gets different signals and produces different sequences and patterns. It stimulates new links in the brain. Rather the thoughts we focus on become real life experiences in our mind. So when we change our thoughts, our mind and brain activity changes too. An intentional mind literally conditions and organizes matter into map of our destiny. See it like this you are trying to lose weight. You are putting the same effort and diet pattern, and yet after a loss of few kilos your weight seems to get stuck at the same number. You have to detoxify and break the plateau in order to continue losing weight. How do you do it? By changing your everyday diet plan. That pushes a different signal to your body and you start losing weight all over again. This is exactly what happens in your brain waves. They get stuck from time to time, losing faith in trying out differently. It needs to be shaken from time to time so that it gets new stimuli and changes happen automatically.

Thoughts have the power of showing themselves on your face. For example, as your thoughts are it gets reflected in your face. If you observe you will see some people with serenity written all over their face and some with shades of distorted anger. A compassionate heart and happy thoughts can only result in a similar frame of mind and vice verse. If your mind is disturbed by lust, jealousy and greed, it can't reflect peace on your face. This is the reason people say face is the mirror of your mind, reflecting directly the state of your mind. Positive thoughts create more happiness and meanwhile negative thoughts like rage, hatred false ego and jealousy can only perpetuate similar feelings. They not only destroy your peace of mind but also disturb the harmony existing around you. Hence to be happy and positive at all times sets a similar feeling chain. A happy mind creates a healthy body but a negative mind can only lead to a sick body, if not physically definitely mentally. Every human being is unique, the thoughts and the mental makeup of each is however different. That is the reason we have differently manifested destiny around us. Not only does our physical energy and strength differ so does the mental capability and strength too. When we take positive stance while crafting our goal, we become stronger in our back up of our faith. We can equally limit ourselves and the possibilities for us by our own self –defeating thoughts.

The thoughts condition our mind and the feelings condition our body. When both are in sync we become ultimate creator. NLP teaches us to be more effective in our own lives. Understanding the foundation pillars will help us to be more effective in our relationships. They are explained as follows-

-<u>RAPPORT</u>- We exist in this world on basis of our relationship with others. They are relationships with people around us and also relation with self by cultivating faith. NLP teaches us to know the boundaries and work effectively within them. When the rapport between us and people related to us becomes smoother it helps in achieving your goals faster.

-<u>SENSORY AWARENESS</u>- If you are alert and aware regarding your senses, your perception of each event in life differs. The theory teaches you to focus with more awareness.

- <u>OUTCOME ORIENTED THINKING</u>- this helps you to focus on what you want, have trust and faith in your inner powers and work towards it accordingly. Until the focus and clarity occur the outcome is compromised.

-<u>BEHAVIOR FLEXIBILITY</u>- flexibility helps in quicker learning and with increased level of rapport the outcome is more positive.

Visualization of Our Reality Change:

When we start questioning our destiny and sit up to question it, this itself is considered as the first positive step towards the change. The questioning arises only when we are in troubled state or are facing hardships. To effect a change that we want to bring about we must first identify what we exactly want. We have to define the goal very clearly to ourselves. As it is a step by step process, every step signifies a small change which manifest at the end as our desired change.

How do you find yourself today? Are you happy or not satisfied with life? Are you happy with where you stand today in your life and your shaping destiny? Do you have faith in the universal powers and your own capabilities? Did you work enough towards achieving your goal and shot it with all the best that you could? If the answers to these are in affirmation, there is no worry. But if they happen to be in negative there are things you get to be doing to make a difference to your future. Your present circumstances may not be to your liking or may have been the result of your own wrong decisions, but if the willingness to change and the awareness to change is present it can be changed. We discussed how thoughts from your mind are the ones to be aware of to modulate any changes. One of the techniques is to do the same with proper intent is Visualization. Is it mere fancy imagination we are talking about? No, we are addressing a need to believe in the reality we want, having faith in it and creating it with our intention.

Every person can use visualization technique or mental imagery to prepare for all situations, however challenging they may be. It is scientifically proved that we can experience both the real imagery and mental imagery in similar ways. For example, when we mentally imagine a picture and believe it to be real even then brain stimulation occurs. These can be recorded to match with others which are recorded when the real imagery is being experienced. When we repeat this a few times do we prepare the brain to be ready when the actual process occurs? To be able to effectively work on visualization we need to be aware of all the five senses to their maximum effectiveness. The practice of the technique needs you to be completely immersed in it to visualize it to be true. Doing the whole exercise step by step in our own mind not only brings us closer to our specific desired goal it also gives you the confidence when it actually needs to be done. Say you are imagining a sunset; you have to make a mental imagery of it, have faith in your abilities, and shoot with everything you have to turn that into a real image on canvas with colors! How strong your faith is depending on how similar both the images are.

Now think of something you would like to see as reality. Once you decide what the thing or desire will be, imagine the same in your mind. With no questions about how it is going to happen or which factors will influence that. This doubt can subconsciously move you away from your picture. So never doubt your faith in your minds power and just have the confidence of seeing through the change.

Walk Towards Your Future:

We all face difficult and unfavorable situations in life, there are moments in time when you just need to hold on to your faith and hope to see through. There is always a way out , out of the darkest of hours, the need is to not get overwhelmed and lose our faith and confidence in the supreme power of god, Universe and that of your own self. We need to cultivate a state of life where our mere existence is also happiness. We need to be able to live in such a way that each moment is joyful and fulfilling. Keeping your faith helps you transcend to that level. If you have goodness in your heart and hold your values well, the conviction in yourself will take you a long way.

The universe is one, we are a part of it and till we learn to align with it. We will also realize that being a success helps others in achieving their life goals if our lives are all interconnected. On the other hand, being a failure or unable to see your desired life circumstances does not help anyone. To be able to work towards your calling with help of our faith in our creator may seem our life goal which we shall reach in the small steps we take. Faith instills us with a power, a "go get 'em tiger" attitude, be it in us, our surroundings, events or gods. It instills us with the capability to turn things better in our way and in the life of the others. So, let us envision a future for ourselves and paint a picture of it in our minds. Ensure the picture you paint is specific, as it is that picture which will be your reality. With our efforts we shall see them unfolding perfectly!

CHAPTER 9: THE POWER OF LANGUAGE WHAT IS LANGUAGE?

Origin of language can be traced back to prehistoric times, when our ancestors were in the form of greater apes. When it came to hunting, fighting the odds of survival or wooing the pretty lady in the group, gestures were introduced to transfer the thought process from one brain to another. We need to explain the other person what we want, and there should be some way that other person understands what we are hinting at. Gestures followed by grunts and noises, and slowly got shaped into assigning every object with a different sound. Those sounds gradually became words, and it did not take much time before using words to denote feelings and emotions.

Language is the system of words or signs that people use to express their thoughts and feelings to each other. The thought which originates from the mind or brain is bare. The mind then works on it to present it in a way as can be understood by another mind and hence covers the thought in chain of words and presents it as language. It is hence way beyond just a means of communication. It is one of the basic ways by which we interact and work together. It is a means of connecting minds for sharing ideas and working on them together. It could be described as assimilation and accumulation of shared meaning, generally of common grounds. A word as language is a human capability and sets us apart from other living animal communications. Animals too can communicate with each other using sounds that may however just appear sounds to us as we do not understand their meaning. If it is not form of language then one dog would not have understood what the other dog means with its bark. Language is processed in many different locations in brain. We are believed to have acquired language and communication through social interactions in early childhood and the human culture cannot be imagined without its existence. Speaking is the way we express language besides sometimes expressing it through signs and gestures too. The scientific study of different languages is called linguistics. We need language in our daily interactions and use it to express our needs, feelings, emotions and use it to question people regarding the same. Without this our basic understanding of the world around us would not be possible. Communication skills- that implies the way you present your thoughts in appropriate words to the other people; also plays an important part in it.

"Language is a process of free creation; its laws and principles are fixed, but the manner in which the principles of generation are used is free and infinitely varied. Even the interpretation and use of words involves a process of free creation. "
NOAM CHOMSKY

We use language to communicate, converse, collaborate and co create. If you were to imagine one day of your life to be spent without being able to express yourself, may be that would be the most torturous day of your existence!!! However, hermits who have isolated their mind from materialistic life spend days in isolation in the world of their own, connecting with spiritual powers above without using language. They don't use language but they communicate. They talk to themselves and the superior powers through meditation and self talk. That's something very powerful and celestial way of expression which is hard to understand for a normal human being. Even when they have discarded language they have a way of expression to the almighty and have greater power than all our "wants" that we express in prayers through words.

Importance and Need of Language:

-It is language which shapes our thoughts and emotions and decides how one would perceive reality. Our common interests and ideas are shared through what we speak. Whether it's interpersonal relationships or they are business relations across countries, they are shared via language.

-Language helps us make bridges in inter personal relationships, making the foundation of our existence. Whether you need to talk to your 5 year old instructing her regarding her school activity; telling your spouse about the weekend family dinner or remind your workmate regarding the early morning meeting. The common thread amongst all is the communication of words between the two parties without which nothing exists.

-Using appropriate language is as important as speaking. We use vivid language when dealing with small children; inclusive language when dealing with special groups and familiar language when jargons need usage in a work setting.

-Using language positively than a negative connotation in anything you say always portrays you in a positive light. Speaking clearly besides the choice of words is also important in interactions.

-Language affects and reflects reality. How do we connect our emotions to words, how do we process and filter things and do we finally decipher the world around us in words understood by us are all reflected in everyday life.

Creating Our Reality:

Our most important tool for making distinctions in various stimuli and creating our reality is language. The reality is what and how we experience any event or situation in life, which may or may not be the reality. As we have discussed before that any reality doesn't function independently. It stands on pillars of our belief system and the language we use to define it. It is influenced by culture, language and other factors too. Every life event and experience change us as it occurs. The neurons in our mind keep making new connections in new situations as an when we are experiencing it. So, any situation which occurs in our life does influence the brain in certain ways. This in turn influences how we understand and relate to concepts presented to us.

For example, as we look around the room where we are seated right now, we see the images and we are talking about everything around to ourselves, through images. Our language is structuring or constructing our reality. Whatever exists around us isn't good or bad –whether it is weather outside, or the pictures on the wall. They become good, bad or any other adjective we attach to it through our perception. The real world just exists but our world develops on the basis of our thoughts, perception and internal judgments'. Let's take an example to understand this concept. Do you remember when you first held your first born in your arms, the world suddenly seemed a different place altogether. There was a spring in your step, your life seemed chirpier, people seemed a lot friendlier and your aches and pains did not matter so much. Did the things really change or just because of your mental state the words you used to define your state through your language, brought about the difference. If as humans we were really in a position to understand the connection between our language and our reality, we would be so conscious and cautious so as to not utter a single inconsequential word drop out of our mouth. Every time we utter a word, whether to ourselves or to others we reveal our own selves through it. The tone you choose to speak, the words you select, your expressions while you speak are all a part of it. The person who then receives it then understands it according to his understanding.

The Concept of Self:

Communication in our life happens as a monologue and dialogue, that is, with self or with other people. There are times when an internal dialogue happens within you, sometimes without your knowledge. These conversations also have a tendency to get distorted, just like any other conversation with somebody else. Since these conversations influence how we see our world and ourselves, it also affects our overall being. For example, if I tell myself the world is a beautiful place, it generally will turn out to be. If we keep the channel of communication clear, our life will turn out more meaningful.

We are a sum total of our thoughts. We are shaped as a result of our interaction with the world as infant, our growing up years and the environment around us. If we are nurtured as children we grow up as nurturing adults. We tend to have a positive self-image and a strong mind. A harsh childhood produces damaged and under confident adults. This constant learning, reacting, judging can really get exhausting sometimes. So, we consciously need to pay attention to keep the processes in a positive mode using positive affirmations and messages. Our conditioning begins the moment we are born. As we go about our life, we go through the conditioning process that has created a mind-set with a tilt towards **I am not's.** You got less satisfactory marks compared to your peers and 'not good' as per your parent's expectations, you declare to yourself, **I am not smart**. You come second in the swimming competition after being first in a number of years and start judging your capabilities by feeling, **I am not talented**. You happen to encounter an ungrateful partner, who chooses her happiness elsewhere ditching you, you are a wonderful person but bald, and therefore conclude that she left me because **I am not attractive and unlovable**. Repetitions like these in your childhood, teenage years and finally adulthood gradually becomes the pillars that defines your core self-concept. That is how then you start defining yourself. If some negative patterns seem to have become a trend in your early life years, they can be worked upon and changed. You become so engrossed in absorbing these negative feelings about yourself through self-talk, that you put your inner self capabilities, qualities and talents at jeopardy. Listening actively plays an important role in this. We tend to passively hear than listen.

Why do we communicate? We indulge in conversation because we have a need for it, to tell our emotions and feelings, to ask for our desires and so on. When we don't share or talk we tend to become alone in the world. Depending on our self-concept our life realities shape. So when we have a negative defining concept of ours, how do we overcome that?

Reshaping Reality through Words:

Words shape our present and our future, language adds texture. And we hardly ever paid any attention to them. Lots of our vocabulary we picked up fortunately or unfortunately, from our care givers, who may not have realized themselves of the impact they were making. They are an interesting force; we express them through speeches, normal talking, and poems and so on. Sometimes our words get us into trouble and other times they also get us out of trouble. It actually does not take too much effort to turn our life around and refurbish our internal vocabulary to a different one that aligns to our authentic self. The **I am not** mental frame needs to be overcome and we begin with our inner world of spirit. The inner world has no boundaries and no restrictions imposed on it. But the outer world has obstacles set by our five senses, and outside factors and hence keeps changing. To generate the awareness that by cultivating emotions in the inner world, in the way we see and express ourselves not getting bogged down by the outside world, is of prime importance. This understanding will help you shake and stir your whole belief system into understanding the fact that we live in the world we create, and we create our world by shaping it in words- language, a means by which we self-talk and change our perspectives and talk outside and bring changes to perspectives of others about us.

Once the understanding dawns, do a thorough search of your inner being and list out the things you want to define your life with. Then begin with making the gradual shift from **I am not** to **I am.** Whatever your designs for your life are **I am** need to be in correspondence with our highest inner self, the almighty himself residing in you. Beginning with your inner dialogue, simply change the words that define yourself. Redefine yourself-image by choosing the positive words you have to reconstruct in your mind. Rewarding your inner self with strength, compliment and love everyday will upgrade yourself worth, self-respect, and self-image in a way that you can feel the divine blessings almost coming true to your life and fulfilling your life's cores desires.

Replace the proclamations and self-affirmations of **I am not** too **I am**. By using the words, **I am** regularly to define our own self and what we are capable of are giving regards and respect to the holy expressions for the Supreme Being that resides inside us. So rather than to malign our supreme being, break the habits which make you do so. All it takes is some self-awareness and lots of self-love and we are good for a turn around. The worst we can ever do to anybody or our own self is to condemn or bring down their identity with mean and demoralizing words, when they make mistakes and even when they go about normal routine in daily interactions.

Dale Carnegie rightly put it in his words, "*Instead of condemning people, let's try to understand them. Let's try to figure out why they do what they do. That is a lot more profitable and intriguing than criticism; and it breeds sympathy, tolerance and kindness*" (Carnegie, 1981). It is more about building your own self and others too in the process than breaking their confidence and self image. To develop and empower is a more satisfying action and to dig into your reservoir to do that is the best. Let us strive to make ourselves the best possible picture of ourselves, through our own words. Simply replace the feeling of *I can't* to *I will.* Instead of *I am incapable* to run a kilometer *say I will give my best as a start and improve as days pass by.* Instead of saying *I am not a peace*, say *I will* make changes to see that peace prevails. Replace *I am unlucky in love* to, *I am lovable* and will find the right person able to respect me in whatever frame I am in right time. In place of always feeling and saying *I am unworthy of happiness*, inculcate the feel that *I will find happiness and bring happiness to others life also*. As we speak we create this circle of reality around us.

Does Language Shape The Way We Think:

Researchers have proved that the structure of language and the language itself influences how we think or understand and conceptualize the world around us. The idea that language and thought are intertwined almost like the double helical DNA structure has existed from across civilizations as early as when Plato opined that, to live our physical world we need to have language as a tool or else it was impossible.

One of the most well-known linguists, Benjamin Lee Whorf, said the words;

"We dissect nature along the lines laid down by our native language. The categories and types that we isolate from the world of phenomena we do not find there because they stare every observer in the face; on the contrary, the world is presented in a kaleidoscope flux of impressions which has to be organized by our minds-and this means largely by the linguistic system of our minds. We cut up nature, organize it into concepts, and ascribe significances as we do, largely because we are parties to an agreement to organize it in to the same picture of Universe, unless their linguistic backgrounds are similar, or can in some way be calibrated."

In words we can understand this states that the structure of a person's first language or native language will have influence on how he goes on to view the world. As a person grows and acquires his language, the language and thought equation is also colored by the culture of the place. The culture of your place would include your beliefs, the lifestyle followed, the growing up influences of people you grew up with. Just like the language development is influenced by your families, your school and the societal group around. Same is the process of your thoughts being influenced by your parents, peers and societal group. A simple example is of a child learning to talk the language, using the words the mother uses in his first speaking ventures. These are his first exposure to acquiring the language and then the circle of exposure increases and more people add their input. By mere observation and interactions around without conscious teaching these are passed on.

How do we think? We think in images, colors, smells and also words. Generally, it is believed to be words. This may tell us that for certain aspects we use words to think. Maybe you think of cake and just the smell or aroma of a freshly baked cake is enough to complete your thought. You do not need words. Hence, we come to the conclusion that though our thoughts are influenced by our language it's more of the labeling and assimilation of it which is affected more. It ends up as a two way process then that how you think influences your language and vice versa. The way you perceive the world may be influenced by certain factors discussed before but there is no evidence that it stops you from thinking certain things outside the spectrum as your exposure and cultural experiences increase.

A child growing up in a metropolitan city in a country will have different thought process, language belief and ideas than a tribal boy in a small village in an underdeveloped country. Even if this boy grows up, acquires education, goes abroad and becomes classmates of the former boy, their personal influences of culture will reflect in the way they see the world and express their beliefs in the same language. Certain young people find it cool to call "my" a two letter word as "mah" a three letter word, similarly "super" as "suppah" and so on. Use of abbreviations is normal as they shrink the word into small size so that it can be written fast and understood by majority. However, in the earlier case it's the influence of the peers or the culture that reflects in the way they write and express their thoughts.

Moving Ahead and Connecting Beyond;

Language being an important aspect of our life needs overall understanding in all its relevance. The world around us consists of thought, energy and vibrations which manifest themselves not only into how our world shapes up it also has the capacity to change it for better. Our language consists of words and thoughts. Thoughts have energy vibrations associated with it. When these vibrations connect to ones present in our universe there is an exchange of energy between them. As the words and inter related thoughts have tremendous power they can be harnessed by attracting similar ones from the universe. We are interlinked with the superior almighty, the universe he created and the life surrounding us. When we think of negative thoughts, we speak negative words. Negative words create hurt and anger to the listener. He again puts that negativity transmitted from you to someone else, slowly like a chain reaction, many people get affected by it. Groups of negative vibes out from people can in turn make a society sour, the atmosphere at large. Imagine a car emitting poisonous gases; he will not make much effect in the road. But a group of cars with high level of poisonous gases can pollute the air. When you set a negative vibe free from you, it gets transmitted from one person to another and eventually like a boomerang comes back to you. Think positive act positive, speak positive, humanity needs it, you need it and the cosmic powers can appreciate it. If this is practiced by connecting to positive vibrations in the universe, we may be surprised to see that it sends in our way reaction of similar kinds. This may result in a better world for us in the longer run.

"No one can touch word, but words can touch everybody. We are masters of unspoken words and slaves of the spoken"- unknown.

By choosing words which connect to the higher truth of world we may ascend in our spiritual growth and advancement. One a word goes out of our mouth it's like an arrow out from the bow. It can never turn back. As we speak we create, we have the power to create an atmosphere of hell or heaven around us. .... let's connect our emotions to our words, kind words can touch and change even an animal. When you give away positivity, kindness, humanity, and love to this world, the world like a sponge accepts it. The universe reflects the same things back to you. This however doesn't mean that you will bestow all these qualities on a person who does not deserve.

RamkrishnaParamhansa, an Indian saint once said *"you need not bite everyone, but make sure to hiss once in a while so that they can understand biting is a choice you are restricting out of your own good"*

It's how you use the words the language and the feeling you connect with the universe that matters at the end of the day. The world is already suffering. Suffering from pride, ego, anger, lust, gluttony, greed, and envy, and unable to think and feel like human, your own efforts may seem like a drop in the vast ocean but be the change you want to see in others.
Say you got verbally abused by your boss in the office. You are upset and go back home. Your wife has put a little too much sugar in the tea. You shout at her, transferring the anger that was inside you to her. She feels bad, in turn when your 18 month old denies wearing a diaper and runs around the house in his own playfulness, without any fault of his, his mother scolds him. So, she too transfers the pent up anger into her child like you did. Negative forces flow from one person to another just like positive forces do. Once a heart breaks be it yours or someone else's it's hard to repair. Start practicing to be positive and you will get back positivity around you. It is important to recognize how powerful positive words and language can be, and start working towards improving your life and relationships through it. Lot of times we do not realize, yet we use metaphors to describe ourselves or may be our life situations, our relationships and so on. What we do not realize is that the impact it has on our lives. For example, if I say "my life's a ride" it may as well become a swell of a ride. if I choose to say" life feels like a jungle" well, it may seem like one and you may well be lost in it!!! Metaphors are embedded in our language and culture more than we can ever imagine. It then becomes important to choose them wisely as they soon start describing and making you feel about it, as you word them. It may just seem a figure of speech yet the power it holds is unimaginable. They are suggestive of how you feel about what you use them to describe, example, Daisy calls

her state of mind always as "over the edge" .... can I blame her if she ends up feeling the same. The mind starts believing the metaphors we use for things, emotions or people over a period of time and starts reacting in same manner. Whenever we realize that we are caught in a routine or pattern and metaphors we use limit our own growth we just need to snap out of it to change them into ones with more positive and spontaneous feel .it does make a difference how we feel about our own selves and also how others perceive us. Hence when we choose our regular with focus and wisely they work and pay off in the long run. Let us leave the disempowering metaphors behind and look towards ones which are nurturing and emotionally connecting and we shall then see the power of words. See and appreciate when you feel a behavior or circumstance that reflects a divine intervention. Have heart to heart talks with inner self and find ways to improve you. You are your best critic; nobody knows your secrets and vices like you do. Ask for forgiveness. Appreciate and respect nature and its beauty. Stop rushing all the time. Stand and smell the roses. Appreciate whatever you got in life, if something was denied, it has its own reasons, maybe it was not worthy of you, maybe something better awaits you. Trust that everyone has ups and downs in life, and if you are going through a down the up will come soon. We need to learn that whatever happens in your mind reflects in our actions, and that affect other people. We have to be careful of what we say and do, as the whole world is not always about us. It's about them, we, and us. We create the world around us. If we make small changes in us, by giving priority to what "I am" capable of doing, it will change the world around us too. "I am" probably the strongest two letter word. For what you put after that becomes your reality. The reality created by you, truer than true, and thus defines your future and destiny. Language helps us connect to our inner world to express what we feel about ourselves. We are our biggest critic. For when we do something wrong, we can escape the law, but not the conscience. So what we believe and what we feel about ourselves, changes the life we live in reality. So if we focus on our strengths and pat our own back from time to time at small achievements, our life will fall back in the right track.

Words work both ways, either they build or they destroy; how we use them will give us the ultimate result. Our words and thoughts almost act like a command to our mind. So let us invest in positive affirmations and thoughts. Positive thoughts create positive words, positive words create positive actions, and positive steps generate positive inventiveness. So, eliminate the negative inside your head to create a positive world around you!

CHAPTER 10: FEAR- THE GREATEST ENEMY

Imagine a normal playtime situation. You are in the park with a group of children, each engrossed in some form of play. A snake is spotted slithering across incidentally in one of the corners, the kids react in awe and curiosity. One of the mom freezes in fear, the security guard handles the situation in time and no harm comes to anyone. Imagine another situation. Andrew is home alone, waiting for his parents to come back. Suddenly there is a sound in the attic, he screams in panic. A common link between both situations is the emotion- Fear. Some have fear of darkness, some of heights, some of hospitals -majority of us have some fear or the other. There are so many types of fears or phobias that exist in the dictionary…and you will be amazed to find so many unusual fears that people find hard to cope up with.

Fight-Or-Flight" Response Of Our Mind:

"What would you do if you were not afraid in life? "Lot of people would think for a while and come up with a response that says *"may be a lot more than what we have done now"*, all because they were afraid of what lay ahead or what would be the result and so on. **Fear** is one of the basic emotions which we all feel, which is induced by a threat perceived by us. This feeling of fear causes a change in brain and organ function and ultimately a change in behavior too. Fear generally occurs in response to a specific stimulus, happening in the present or something that will occur in the future. This perceived situation is taken as threat to life, health, work or anything valuable in life. When a stimulus is received which induces fear in our mind there are two general reactions that occur. Either we see the

situation and run away from it, trying to avoid it and thinking it would go away. Or we counter the situation and respond to it as our mind or brain asks us to respond to it. These two reactions make our so called **"Fighter-Flight"** response of our mind. Fears are judged as natural or rational fears and inappropriate or irrational fears. An irrational fear is termed as phobia. Fear is not an external factor, it is an innate ability which has been developed as an internal system required for our survival, and even the process of evolution supported it. And hence it stayed as a part of our existence from time immemorial. However, we may try to delete it from our lives there are manifestations of it in our daily lives. When the emotion is felt within limited levels, we see through it but when it increases to a size much bigger it becomes difficult to handle. It is this situation that we need to deal with it because it hinders our growth and stops us from moving forward in life.

Alice may be afraid of spiders, she may shriek or shout and somehow kill or shoo away the thing and get away with it. This fear is not hindering her life process in any way; but Andrew may be afraid of public speaking, whenever he sees different faces in front and he is made to speak up or present something he starts to sweat and stammer. This may be disastrous for his professional growth. Fears like this need to be handled wisely to grow and stand out in a crowd. Or all your efforts will lie in vain and someone less worthy and more confident may win the crown. Another person may be afraid of heights, if probed further you will also find that this person will surely encountered dreams in which he is falling from a height. It's an indication of insecurities, instabilities and anxieties that are very much present in real life. A person like that needs physiologically analyzed. The fears are a manifestation of his mindset that he finds hard to deal with. You will never find a child afraid of anything. It's because its lack of experience in life that he is yet to be afraid of something. You can see a child trying to hold a street dogs tail without being afraid of it, as he has never been bit or seen a dog bite someone. On the contrary being a mom, you will nearly have a heart attack to see your child behave in that manner because of your past encounters with untamed dogs and know how dangerous they can be. Fear is in the mind. It stops you from doing something that you experience in life situation, killing the probability that, that particular dog may be extremely friendly and loves kids and will no way harm it in any way. You pelt a stone and shoo away the dog, when the dog could have been your child's best friend.

We could also explain fear as thoughts that we have in mind or what we think, when we are faced with a negative or defeating experience. When we experience the event or situation, we reinforce that feeling and emotion again on our mind trying to analyze it and see through its impact on our lives. In a way with the mind reading the same feeling repeatedly, develops a fearful response to it. The response is imprinted on it for further reference. This proves that *fear is a learnt response or reaction, then a natural instinct.* It is a creation of our mind so the good news is it can also be un-learnt or overcome by it. For example, when we burn our hands in a freak accident in a gas stove fire while working in kitchen, the first instinct after the initial pain is fear in our mind. Not only are we hurt in the experience, it takes a while to start functioning normally again. It's always working at the back of your mind. You analyze how it happened, how we could have avoided it and how much stress it caused you in the process. By indulging in these thoughts, you are only reinforcing in your mind that fire can cause mishaps and it could be a bigger one next time and it is better to avoid being in same situation, the mind develops a fear in the meantime. This disturbs your mind and your general harmony in the way. If such fear is controlled right at the beginning by logical reasoning that it was a mishap and could have happened to anybody. If you rather feed the fear and start thinking worse situations of similar kinds then it will get out of control of your own mind and start causing issues while you work. The thoughts drain your nervous system and lower your energy, making you vulnerable. Fear has the quality of wrapping around you and engulfing you, it tries to close you down.

Our brain is a complex organ. It comprises of an intricate network of communication between billions of nerve cells. These nerve cells are the beginning point of all the sensory actions, our thoughts and experiences. Fear also is a chain reaction occurring amongst them.

When we were younger we were always told to do this and to not do that, we generally followed those instructions. If we didn't we were punished rebuked or shamed. Since our lives are dominated by two basic motivating forces, which are love and fear our actions are generally based on this duality of love and fear. We are afraid of so many things in life. It may be death, failure, humiliation and so on. What do we do about these fears which we hold in life? Fear like other emotions is linked to energy too, is explained as a contracting energy. If the feeling of fear repeats itself again and again, it becomes a habit in the mind and its reactions a habit in the body. These reactions of fear start living in our body without our knowledge and stay there till they overwhelm and need to be treated. Just like thought attracting one of similar kind in universe, so it is with fear. This emotion attracts situations of similar kind. The habit of this negative emotion needs to be broken or overcome. It is easier to give in to your fears and feel sorry about yourself, than trying to overcome them. That's always the easy way out isn't it? They seem so ingrained that breaking them looks like a huge uphill task. But the sooner we understand that they are more of illusions created by mind, everything is in our head, the easier it gets to break the negative connotation and overcome the feeling.

What Causes Fear In Our Minds?

Fear is a chain reaction caused by a stimulus and ending in a physical response to it. Fear acts instantly, even before we are able to think about it. A large part of fear is a response to the horror of painful experiences of life and besides that also leads to many subconscious behaviors which are known much later. It makes people nervous, anxious, and worried and also interferes with their thinking ability and body functions. This is a negative and unpleasant reaction lot of us would like to avoid but it has its positives too. If fear didn't exist we may do a lot of things which would put our life in danger. It would tell our mind to be cautious in times of threat to keep us safe.

Few of our fears are external fears, that is, the stimulus has been an external agent or an experience from past, through learning and is called fear conditioning. Say you fell into a pit and were eventually rescued later. But your mind will be programmed in those few stuck hours in a way that you will start being afraid of heights, (acrophobia), fear of enclosed spaces (claustrophobia) or fear of falling (bathophobia).

Again a few of them are internal fear which develops due to inadequacies in our core system or internal system. Low self esteem can be a trigger for this. For example, a child who has had more of criticism and harshness during growing up years will have insecurity, showing up as fear in certain life requisites. These inadequacies show up as fear of failure, fear of rejection, fear of having relationships etc. in later part of life.

Eva was a cheerful child, yet extremely shy and this would manifest in extremes like not talking to people at all in the first interaction. As and when the psychologist worked with her over months it was discovered that the child was very wary of talking. She would be admonished at all times at home for talking more than her share and sometimes also being asked to keep shut as a punishment. Her inherent nature of expressing herself through emotions got setbacks again and again. This slowly developed into a fear of talking or interacting with people, for if known people would treat her like that, she felt what would unknown people feel about her? In internal fears like these the mind assumes a particular response and action from external factors and this hypothetical situation restricts his ability to explore experience and step ahead to try and see what the situation really holds for them.

Sometimes the fear arises out of ignorance or lack of information. When you do not have full knowledge about an event or thing, we tend to worry about it and start putting two and two together. We are afraid of stepping into the unknown. This leads to unnecessary fear in our lives. Fear in bearable limits has never been a cause of concern, it is when it starts to manifest in all areas of life and starts to hamper normal functioning it needs assessment for concern and confrontation.

Phobias:

Maria sees a spider, anywhere in front of her – she is unable to react normal. She goes into a crazy frenzy trying to drive it away. She screams in fear, runs around calling for people to help her and sweats profusely till the spider is driven away and out of her sight. The reaction of the person is illogical and the fear not appropriate to the danger. This is an example of Phobia called arachnophobia.

Phobia is described as irrational fear. There are so many numbers of phobias that are found. The person has unending fear towards a situation, some creature, places or things. In these cases, the mind perceives the expected threat to be much more than it actually is. It brings on high degrees of distress and puts obstacles in normal functioning of people.

They are generally described as simple or specific phobia. They are related to things, people, place, animals, things etc. The other category is the complex phobia, which are based on psychological mindset of people or their traits. Social phobia and agoraphobia are examples of this. When you are surrounded by fear it starts to paralyze you. For example, if someone has a fear of elevators. He may be claustrophobic. A history of being locked up in bathroom maybe as a child given as a punishment? You do things in such a way that the situation to travel by elevator does not arise. But is it possible that such a situation will not arise. So, you start avoiding the hour when it is empty. You go late to work, so that the elevator is always crowded. Things go fine until your boss wants you to accompany her to a meeting. The meeting is important but the need to travel in elevator puts the extreme fear and do not go to work that particular day, you call in sick. How many times can you do that? With a combination of all factors and your behavior at work you are not going to be kept for long at work!

When the fear goes out of manageable limit it needs intervention. It is extremely exhausting and upsetting to feel extreme fear that goes with a phobia. People become so stuck that they start losing out on opportunities because of this condition. When life starts getting paralyzed due to fear, it is time to confront them to deal with them and find back the balance in life. It is a very difficult task yet with the willingness, it can be done. There is only one way to overcome fear and that is to confront it. The more times we give in to our fears the stronger it becomes and harder to overcome. When we do the opposite and start to stand up against our fears it gets weaker in strength and a lot easier in overcoming it.

Ten Things That Fear Works On You!

Fear restricts our ability to try out things and be in places or situations which we did not encounter. Our past experiences and opinions cloud our judgment and we follow a pattern that given 2+2 only four can happen. We forget that 1+3 can also give us 4. Here are some ways that fear condition our reasoning:

1. Fear reduces our capacity to give our best by assuming our worth. It makes us lose our faith in us and stands in our path of building our "I am"

2. Fear makes us take wrong decisions in life, well not always, but then unless you taste the ice cream you would really not know whether it's sour or sweet.
3. Fear destroys our voice, we keep mum and lose out on opportunities when we should speak up and claim our worth.
4. Fear makes us prey to others opinion when we should rely on the inner power of us. The typical *"what will people think?"*
5. It helps you to keep away things that are broken, misfit and harmful away from you, as if you were as forgiving as what they call as god, your life would actually have been quite messy!

6. Fear causes us not to embrace change and makes us comfortable with the usual. We are so comfortable to the situation that we presently are in that we fear to explore. Just think exactly how many excuses you have given yourself from the weight loss goals everyday telling yourself that it will be done from tomorrow?

7. Due to fear of losing control or being perfectionist, we fear to assign delegate and give a part of our duties and responsibilities to others fearing its quality. We all feel somewhere that "no one can do it better than me". And it's the irrational fear to lose out on control that we get ourselves overburdened.

8. Fear makes us lie and commit more sins and crimes even by trying to shield someone or us from something. When we should try and get help, we resort to unlawful means!

9. We fear complications and difficulties and avoid responsibilities. We see a road accident, but do not offer help fearing legal complications and other obligations when it's our responsibility to help the needy.

10. Fear makes us take the easy way out rather than taking the right step. The difficult road is always the right one, most often, there may be exceptions though and fearing the long turn of paths we do what we simply feel should help us at that moment rather than thinking about things in the long run.

These are not all but just some of the ways that fear holds us back from giving our best. Unless we overcome our fears and stand up for the best and right we can never attain mental peace. Somewhere in the deepest of our conscience this thing will prick us and it's the greatest law court of our life.

Fear Distorts Our Perception and Distorts Reality:

When people exist in long periods of constant fear, whether it is from physical threat in the surroundings or it is perceived threat in mind, they become stuck or incapacitated. When body senses danger it produces hormones and sharpens functions for survival. Once these reactions start to occur, the brain becomes overactive and stores information in a chaotic way, confused by some mixed signals. Later brain works on those signals and takes them as triggers for a chain of fear reactions, challenging rational thinking. This continuous threat weakens our immune system and cause damage to heart. Gastrointestinal issues like irritable bowel syndrome come up. Changed brain activity leaves the person anxious all the time. Fear also creates obstacles in our brain processes and impacts our thinking and decision making. All the aspects of our individual existence are under impact.

Not many understand that fear distorts perception. It runs like a projector in your mind and shows you pictures through the fear shaded glass, without you even realizing it. It tries to convince you of things that do not even exist. It may you run from situations by believing that it is the right response, when it may be the last option you may have ever weighed. It is human condition to fight fear and it works in unique ways. Sometimes in intimate relationships, where there should be love there is an unexplained fear lurking in the background. The fear of rejection, the fear of getting hurt, fear of invasion, fear of performance, fear to qualify as being perfect and so many others cloud the process and mar the moment of its uniqueness. For example, James is in a relationship for 3 years. They are waiting to take it to next level of marriage. The love which binds them together suddenly sends ripples of fear in his mind. *"Is she the one for me?"* *"Why isn't she more spontaneous?"*, *"why doesn't she do anything special for me?"*, *"is there anyone else?* "and the questions start occurring in his mind. Just the mere fact of loving someone brings in an element of vulnerability. One can confuse these as fear of commitment. It makes you doubt in fear as to where the relationship is headed. You may in such situation pick on your partner with smallest of reason and get irritated for no apparent reason. As the issues increase it makes him to believe that it is better for them to go separate ways. It is just a friend's intervention of seeking a counselor as a last pitch to saving their relationship that saves them from walking the wrong way. With fear thrown out of picture, clarity and love prevails and let them again see each other as they are. See here what they were doing is not the right thing to do, but the easy way out. This intervention makes them understand that it is their partner they would like to live the life with and no one else. Love is a stronger emotion than fear, and therefore the later was ruled out. A simple example of how fear could have destroyed a beautiful relationship with wrong perceptions.

Our perceptions are so important to us, but if the perception gets compromised our reality differs. Perceptions at times get clouded by certain fears we hold, anger in our system towards certain people or situations or guilt playing a victim somewhere in mind. When this happens we start missing clues in our own environment and details are lost without our catching it. This decreases the accuracy of our perception. Hence it is important to identify when it is getting distorted and consciously move out the triggers out of your life. Chose the right feelings to see reality as it is.

Reality distortion happens in different ways in different people. The causes though are not very clear. Anxiety sets the brain in a pattern or set of reactions which are away from the need of the hour. People feel confused at the time and are unable to take proper decisions. Few people just stop processing the outside information. Some people feel something wrong in their lives and yet cannot make out what it is. Sometimes anxiety overpowers so much that our mind is distressed and distracted by unusual thoughts. The emotion of fear gets manifested as certain physical symptoms too. Few people show aggressive behavior and few go completely frozen by fear unable to react. Say your 14 year old declares that she is pregnant; father's response slapping the girl hard on the face; mother's response freezing and unable to react. Both have different or same fears, but process differently. It causes an obstacle in the way of progress by not allowing paying more importance to the need of the hour and taking the right decisions accordingly.

Few common symptoms we see around us in our lives could be these-
Rapid breathing, increased pulse rate, sweating, wide eyes and dry mouth, shaking of hands, unable to move are some of them. Some related behaviors also manifest as ways of executing the symptoms of fear. Sleep and appetite disturbances, crying often without any valid reason, absentmindedness is different ways of your body informing us that there

is something wrong with it. When such occurrences start happening on a more than regular basis, it is needed to get it evaluated by someone specially informed of the field. Extreme fear, anxiety depression and hyper sensitiveness to any situation are all closely inter connected and need to be addressed so that they don't get a hold on your life.

Overcoming Fear and Drawing Strength from Within:

*"**I** am sitting at home, bracing myself for a day at work. There is an important presentation in my department. I am required to begin the same and then handover to my team mates to carry further. The opening remarks are all ready and I have seen them number of times. Yet I sit there, trying to catch my shallow breath, with a definite unease in my chest. I do not know what is happening to me and I do not know what to do."*

These are words of Alice, a 25 year old. How terrifying can a situation like this be in life and how long can anyone sustain life like this. Sooner or later the system will collapse, if the person is not assessed immediately.

Fear and anxiety are a part of our lives. Our wellbeing and survival depends on it, so we are wired accordingly. They cannot be eliminated from our system completely. The only need is to regulate the degree of fear we feel. We need to develop strategies to cope when need be. When the fear levels go beyond normal and start interfering in your day today life that it is a cause of worry. Even the most brilliant of minds and most courageous of hearts have been overwhelmed by fear at some point in their lives. Some people are afraid of tangible things and some are afraid of things that cannot be seen.

We have to go about bring the change in us from being fearful to fearless in a methodical way. The following methods could be enlisted in the process:

-**Evaluate your fear**- It's always easy to be in denial than to confront, so lot of us avoid looking at them too. But confronting is the first step to dealing with it. Acknowledge the existence of your fear. Maybe write it down to give it a face. Try and find the source and the history of your fear. What are the triggers? Are the fears real enough? Move to the next step of the goal or the thing you want to change. Break the ultimate goal into small steps and start working.

-**Get in control of your fear**- we generally have fears about which we don't have enough information. If we instead expose ourselves to it in small ways we are more aware of it. Other option is to go into your fear head on. You can either overcome or give in. if you conquer, repeat again.

-**Change your way of thinking**- Start by seeing your fear in a different light. Instead of a negative take treat it as learning or an opportunity to correct something in your own life. For example: the fear of water once overcome can lead you to go on boat trips and go for regular swimming like your mates. This itself should motivate you to work towards it.

-**Let fear have a place in life**- Fear has to be a part of our life. Everyone has some or the other fears. It's okay to accept to yourself that there are some and not be too critical of yourself. They can be overcome. It may take time and effort yet can be done. But as you go along, each step you take in positive direction should be rejoiced. Since each one is a step towards your desired goal. Be proud in accepting that. Sometimes fear are for good. You may be afraid of speed. It's okay to keep this fear as long as it's allowing you to have a life of your own. If it's not letting you go for those long drives with your partner it's wrong, but if it's making you a cautious driver preventing you from reckless driving, it's actually helping you in a way and therefore should be kept.

Empowering Self:

It always pays to be prepared in life; challenges generally don't have a habit of announcing before they come!! Rather than to be tested for difficult situations and then rising out of them it makes more sense that you are empowered beforehand in case anything strikes. There are certain effective techniques and steps which any of us can take to reduce the negative impact on our lives with the threat of fear on it.

-**Exercise and fitness**: believe it or not, the studies have found that following an exercise routine and having good cardiovascular fitness goes a long way in reducing effects of fear and anxiety. It makes you stronger in facing anything that comes your way.

-**Positive mindset**: when we tune our mind to positive thoughts and affirmations, it changes the way we think and the thoughts we produce. Fears are after all thoughts and notions produced in mind and if we reinforce thoughts which enable us to feel we can overcome and keep us motivated, we are less anxious.

-**Change of perspective:** we are always daunted by the impact of any negative occurrence or event. We never bother to see the bigger picture, and how maybe the event helped us in some areas of life. Our tire punctures and we are unable to go to office in time and are afraid of facing our boss, what we did not realize is if we were in time, we would have met a road accident that someone else encountered.   It helps a lot when we change the way we approach fear and its consequences. For example, rather than being bogged down by the immediate reaction of people around at a public address, if you fail think what happens if all goes well. The claps and cheers will momentarily give you the frame of mind to go ahead and do the job well.   Keep the best and worst case scenario in head, and charge ahead.

-**Close net of friends:** we are social beings and our survival depends on interactions with the others. Any challenge that crops up in our life can be handled well with the support of friends. Friends can be a great support system as they are the ones who know us truly. Friends help us get over our fears by pushing us to go ahead and just do it. Close friends are always there to give us advice when we are trying to get over some fear. Remember when you feel a door is closed and afraid to enter, it may just need your push to open it again. And great friends can give you that push required to overcome fear.

-Climb one stair at a time: sometimes the fears are so big that overcoming them seems impossible. Yet when we break the same into steps, they are dealt with better. Focus on them one by one to move ahead steadily. Make small achievable targets and move steadily. Don't make plans that are not only impossible to achieve but will completely blow away your confidence when not done. See a child. First it crawls, it is afraid to walk without support, then takes the initiative of first few independent steps, feels confident, sometimes falls, but yet continues to walk, and in a few days, start running all over the house.

-Challenge self: when we challenge our own self by setting the same fears to be conquered. We begin by doing similar things at smaller scale and then push boundaries slowly. The brain gets the signal of a positive outcome. The brain then gets accustomed to such challenges and then keeps on pushing itself to conquer them. Do not get opinionated by what others feel or tell you about. The only person worth having competition is your past. Always compare your past and ask yourself have you reached a little closer to your goal than yesterday? If yes, then you know you are in the right direction. Always congratulate yourself in front of the mirror for challenging yourself and achieving your little targets. That way you stay focused on your path to success and do not let irrational fear fog your way.

Majority of us think of fear in a negative connotation, something we would rather avoid. The world sometimes seems a scary place to survive if we have to live in fear every day. By allowing it to rule over us we allow it to stop us from achieving a lot of goals we had set for ourselves. But we sometimes fail to understand that fear also has surprisingly positive effects as well. This emotion has been ingrained in us for survival and can bring out abilities we were unaware of existed within us. We have to believe that that the intent with which we are sending our thoughts to overcome something is pure. This is then sent out with complete faith that what you desire will come through. Allow then your mind to take over and focus on it to be achieved. There are reserves each human being holds within. Sometimes fear is the emotion which taps it to forefront in a crisis. Let us not be conquered by fear, let us instead conquer fear instead.

CHAPTER 11: HOW YOUR MEDITATION AND PRAYERS HELP YOU ACHIEVE

We live in a world today which is so torn apart by anger, ego hassles, hatred and rivalry. Our life is a mixed bag of good and bad, of happiness and sorrow, of success and failure and that of highs and lows. There are times when we can get lost and confused in times of chaos. We have self-doubts that are our greatest enemy. No matter what we do we cannot find peace of mind. Mental ailments in everyday stressful lives are becoming normal. That is the time when we need to just become still and go within to regain our strength through surrendering and meditation. This reflection more than anything else connects you to your own self which tends to get neglected and overlooked in the fast pace of today's lives.

Challenges and problems are bound to come in our lives. Before they unravel and engulf you, take your own time to build yourself stronger. This can only be achieved through meditation. Meditation doesn't mean always praying to god to make everything all right in our lives. It's connecting to the inner peace, inner self and inner potentials and strengths to fight back the negatives that come in our life daily. By paying attention to how we feel, why we feel so and how we can feel different is the endeavor of our minds. Our mind is not only the generator of our thoughts but also the culmination of our thoughts. So, it is on us to regulate the instrument of mind with the right input and output of thoughts. When we choose our thoughts, we manage our own vibrations that are being sent to the universe. Since we are the creator, the onus is on us. We are bigger and stronger than any habit or circumstance.

When we are centered in confusion and chaos, which has become the norm of today's existence, our thoughts too follow the same trend. This leads to our reality being the way it is. When things don't happen the way they should, or life feels stuck in certain situations or even when all seems well and controlled in life we need to realize that a a moment must be spared to reflect and ponder and concentrate on how to change things differently. We must have gratitude to others and life for giving us the power of what we are today and only way to be content and attain inner peace is to connect with your own self and introspect through meditation. It is through prayers, meditation and compassion towards others can we work towards attaining peace. You and I should take initiative to make life happy. Our actions in life should be such that that while we fulfill the need of our lives, they give happiness to those around you.

We are social beings and our existence is dependent on people around us. So, our happiness and peace can only be achieved if we are peace with others besides being at peace with others. When we meditate it gives us the strength not only to see the wrongs that happened to us, or what we did wrong, but also give us the push to act better and make changes to undo the wrongs that caused pain and suffering. Maybe we could have kept a little more patience to feed a two year old. Maybe we could have shown more sympathy to the road side beggar, maybe we could have been more understanding to our employees need for leave application. All these things will come rushing to you, and you will realize, how making little changes in your temperament, attitude and look towards life you can make a hell lot of difference in lives of others and you. When we wake up every day, if we just take a moment to think about what a privilege it is to simply be alive and healthy, life feels different. If we start considering life as a blessing you will start feeling the same. If you start taking life as a journey to be done since you have taken birth, it will feel so. It is hence a matter of attitude and your mindset in life that decides a lot of things in making our reality. Concentrating on your inner self through meditation will empower you to deal with the problems in a more patient and understanding way. It will not help you teach to run away from responsibilities and avoid problems, but will give you the strength to overcome obstacles, give the power to combat ones more effectively and positively when they arise in life, and most importantly help you heal from inside for everything that went wrong for you. Meditating helps you stop regretting about past, being carried away by negative emotions, handle anger and despair maturely and stop us from fretting about the unseen future. Whatever comes our way in future will be handled more positively. It's like sharpening the knife of the mind. The more you do, the more you will be active sharp and alert in life and not let anyone bog you down with their negativity.

Why The Need To Meditate:

Alan always had this idea that meditation was a practice meant only for those desiring to walk on spiritual path, moving beyond the material world we are all stuck in. It seemed very weird even trying to focus on something which you can't see. Jessica on the other hand started with meditation for two minutes thinking what can two minutes do. The curiosity lead to the discovery to a changed human being. The effects of the process were not tangible for all to see or even for self to be motivated with. This precisely is the mindset of all human beings when the questions regarding meditation crop up in our conversations and our lives as such. When do you begin, why do we need it and who do we regard this as our teacher in this journey? Is there a right time? Who informs you that you need it to put a different perspective in mind? Do I need a spiritual guru to start with or can it be done alone? All these questions are bound to come up.

Man has evolved into an independent and capable being where he can sustain himself on his own. But as we take the journey of life there comes a period where you start feeling the need to depend on someone and take care of the bigger picture of your life and keep it enchanting and beautiful. We start praying to god. It just feels nice to believe that god will guide and help us navigate through our problems. We overlook the inner voice for that is a powerful tool god uses to speak to us. Our mind is so distracted with a million outside things that we are unable to concentrate and look within for answers. The soul always knows what to do as its intimate with the divine all the time. Divinity is within us, the secret is to silence the mind so that we can hear our soul speaking what we hold as true in our heart of hearts. Life is like a maze and there are corners and turns where there are chances of getting lost. There are distressing moments, there are rewarding moments, there are also times when things seem to overwhelm you. Times like these, direct you as a person into the practice of meditation. Channels of reaching meditation as a practice to pursue differ. Very few of us take a conscious decision ourselves. We wait till either a situation or a person pushes us, motivates us or coaxes us to motivate. For some it is the Doctor's advice for helping us recover from a mental health issue, for some it is a friend's advice to lower stress. For some it is the well meaning colleague sending you to meditate in some holistic living classes to overcome negative emotions in life such as anger, enmity, and revenge and so on. It seems very rare to come across people who decide to do it on their own, even when all is well, to undertake the practice of meditation. They do it to seek clarity in life, learn to focus and listen to intuition and seek a better quality of life with better relationships. Though the practice of meditation has existed for years immemorial, it becomes the focus of people for different reasons and at different stages of life. The goal for all meditates remains the same- to be able to become more aware and to develop consciousness. They realize that it is a method of personal growth and a tool which we use to our benefit in numerous ways and to a tremendous extent.

Have you ever thought why we clean our house? Well, to keep it clean, so that we feel nice and tidy and fresh all the time right? If your house is clean we work better in it, our productivity is high around the house then. There is no clutter and therefore positivity flows in. Our body almost resembles a house or a room which comes in contact with numerous things. Everyday interactions in and around us create a lot of junk. Junk in form of unwanted emotions, thoughts and feelings accumulate within us. We don't need them yet they are there. Meditation is one way of cleaning your mind and body in an effective way. As we are aligned to our inner being, our awareness becomes stronger. We become less judgmental and focus and pay attention to things that need our attention for our inner growth and which we have neglected all the way as we were very busy doing a thousand other things! To one a business deal may be more important, to another the parent's teachers meet. Both can be stressed in their own way and judge each other for their choices. It's a matter of priorities and believe in me when I say that meditation helps you focus on what is more important to you, what brings you happiness and peace rather than being subjected as victims to another's opinion about you. You will know effectively how to balance the different priorities in life.

When we set course on our spiritual growth, we realize the first thing that comes out of mind is prayers. It comes out then as a natural intent than a mechanically done deed, as we usually do. We send our prayers as a duty to show gratitude and also for our psychological health. Our prayers go out generally with the purpose of requesting help and guidance from the divine. Some do it every day; some do it weekly, some do it before going to bed and meals, while some remember to offer gratitude only before various exams in life, a fast recovery from a disease for self and the list is endless!!! What happens when we pray without any purpose? Maybe just to feel content and show our gratitude's at peace with ourselves. When we do not ask him any material or tangible thing and just allow him to connect with our spirit and guide us in our course of action. What will happen if we can listen to our inner voice, and get a surreal kind of energy and contentment to flow in us, that empowers us enough to tackle things in a more balanced and positive way? We ponder too much on what lies before us and what we left behind. In this way we are depending on outside powers to help us, but the thing is, the power to self help lies within, our spirit knows all the answers, we just need to listen to it.

Meditation and Brain Activity:

What exactly is meditation? Meditation is defined as" *a practice in which an individual train the mind or induces a mode of consciousness to realize some benefit or for the mind to simply acknowledge its contents or an end in itself.*" It can also be

154

understood as a practice of deep consciousness of mind. When a person sits to meditate, the mind stops its obsessive churning and begins to slow down. Your body gets rest when you sleep. Your mind gets rest when you meditate. You feel your attention turning from outside to within. If it is done on a regular basis, it brings about a change in the way we experience our life. It is even found to bring about a change in brain activity and state. Scientists believe that whatever we do and experience in life alters our brain. When people meditate they teach the brain to function in a different way. Meditation is like learning a skill, which comes with learning and practice. When the brain or our mind meditates it develops new and stronger cell connections and restructures it for better processing of matter. Our brain keeps getting sculptured every moment.

We stand to gain a lot of things when we learn to meditate on a regular basis. Few are classified for our understanding.

- IMPROVES ATTENTION – research in recent years have shown that meditation helps in improving concentration. It does so by increasing your focus and also by being more aware of our immediate happenings around us. For example, when our awareness is more the way you experience life differs. By such conditions our experience of any event or relationship improves as you are completely there.

- REDUCTION IN STRESS LEVELS- lots of negative thoughts are ingrained in our minds without our knowledge. They crop up when we least need them and create defeating situations in our lives. Such events can only induce stress. While we learn to meditate we become an observer in the whole situation. As an observer, you become detached and it is easier to process thoughts clearly. The mind feels calmer and you feel more present dealing with life events, this reduces stress. Anytime you feel stress rising, you just quietly focus on your breathing. As you breathe- in and breathe-out, affirm that you calm your mind with inhale and stabilize the feeling with the exhale.

- COMPASSION TOWARDS OTHERS- As we live our lives in stressed states we somehow become oblivious to others and their day today happenings. We are preoccupied by our own sense of struggle and fail to recognize the pain and suffering of others. But with meditation and a comparatively calm state of mind you tend to care more. You are kinder in approach. You tend to lend a helping hand when you see someone in distress.

  This in turn lifts your spirits and the cycle of kindness moves on.
- PHYSICAL BENEFITS- tension related aches and pains go away and the immune system becomes stronger. The energy levels are higher than before as your negative energies are not stifling the positive ones.
- MENTAL BENEFITS- as the mind feels alert and fresh, the anxieties disappear and the feeling of well being and happiness increases. It improves memory recall and overall memories, since the distractions around are cut off. Creativity takes a leap in manifesting. Emotional well being is at better state than before.

Life holds numerous difficulties and tests, or problems as we address them. The majority of them are illusions of mind. Challenges will keep cropping up in different forms. Some injury out of the blue, the insurance payment at the wrong side of month, some disagreement in an intimate relationship, the list goes on. So what do we do? Run out for help, well, NO. Go within to accumulate your own strength. Every issue that arises holds an opportunity in hand; it waits for us to utilize it. It is we who are unable to see it disguised form since our mind is not trained to do so. When the problems occur, our mind is always ready to throw up some excuse or the other to delay or stop any change that needs to occur. It is the same with meditation. But when we finally give in to the practice of meditation we realize that it takes us to different levels of experiencing life. We not only heal from within, we see the interconnections with people around us and become more sensitive to their trials. It is then time to leave all apprehensions and begin learning the practice.

Techniques of Meditation:

We are about to learn a skill to enable us to train and master our thoughts and our mind. Our past, our future and their related thoughts therein take away our present moment. Hence to be in the present moment needs practice and effort. Just imagine a situation. You pick up a book you have been long waiting to read and sit down to read it. You suddenly realize time just flew while you were engrossed in its pages. You were in a timeless space at that point of time. How did this happen? The activity completely consumed you and your mind. Both were in sync with each other, hence the experience was so satisfying and brilliant. Sometimes painting a picture and seeing it through in all sense somehow feels the same. This also is a form of meditation. And if you have been indulging in a hobby like this, you already are practicing meditation in a way. Just letting your mind be away from the distractions of life and focusing or getting engrossed in one mind activity that calms relaxes and satisfied your soul. Let us just etch out how we shall go about the start of meditating process:

- Deciding on a time is very crucial- in our hectic lives time is premium. So find time and decide on a schedule to pursue the practice. If you have time to breathe you can also find time to meditate.

- Comfortable positioning- you must be at ease as you sit in whichever posture you chose. Comfortable environment and surroundings always aid in the process. It should be distraction free as much as possible, allowing you to concentrate honestly.

- Still the mind- begins by being calm and still your mind of any rush. Focus on any object in your mind. If you need a mantra to do it, you can. Try to shove out all thoughts that creep in from all sides in your mind. Make it blank.

- Focus on your breath- as you have already focused on an object in mind, just move to your breath. Feel yourself inhaling and exhaling, by doing this you shut out other thoughts and distractions. In case you need the aid of music in this you can. When mind is in tune with what you tell it to do, it becomes an observer. Your capacity to process any issue related to your life increases.

- Hold the moment of stillness. This is how you broadly move into the zone of meditating; you may begin with few minutes every day and then increase it. If you feel the need of a mentor you can find a learned soul in the field. When benefits of meditation and prayer combine together it gives an increased sense of fulfillment in life. You seem to have more control over your own self, have a positive and compassionate outlook towards all. Everyday living becomes a better experience.

Meditation Touching Various Spheres of Our Lives:

Technology Influencing Humanity:

In the past few decades we have been bombarded with technological advancements in our lives. We exist in times and age where technology surrounds and impacts our lives in innumerable ways. From a corporate person to a toddler, everyone in a victim of technological advances; the way technology manifests in certain ways we might as well wonder …. Whether technology is influencing humans or is it the other way around?

Our definition of humanity, that is, of being human in nature seems to be evolving with technology influences. Human nature defines certain set patterns of thinking, feeling and reacting and so on including trademarks of being human. Technological intrusions seem to be changing these in much bigger ways, than we can imagine. The increasing connectivity in human network through media is at an amazingly high rate. After flooding the social field, it is moving in other areas like organizational set ups, long held human belief systems etc. All this is pushing a change in our societal set up and how we interact. Humanity has belief systems which are hundreds of years old and some of them have evolved through times. Our individual belief systems influence the collective belief system of the society and vice versa. There is an inter change happening at every possible juncture. Technology provides an added angle of interaction between them. There are advancement in cloning of individuals and brain chips and transplants that make human robots and actions are controlled by others in military. Mind power is amazing thing when it comes to controlling of thoughts. Soldiers who were wired have proved to do what humanity called them to do at the need of the hour rather than following orders. If your mind is strong which can be done with regular practice of meditation, you will even be less prone to hypnotism and mind control. Technology has given us also ways to see videos about meditation, spiritual world links that can be useful by ourselves to attain nirvana! Sci-fi films are also imaginations of some mind, someday then can come true, but the mind will remain the biggest machine ever. Mind creates thoughts, and thoughts define us. By empowering our minds, we can challenge even the biggest technological advancements.

Technological advancements though have provided human history directionality, it remains to be seen as the outlook it takes — positive or negative, with regard to humanity. The technological advancements always reverse and rearrange our societal situations. The intrusion of technology seems to be eating into human interactions due to time constraints, different interfaces of interaction and over independence on it. We may take solace in the fact that technology itself is all a invention of human kind and would have not been there if it weren't for the mind power and imagination of it. So we believe that artificial intelligence cannot supersede human intelligence. If the intent of human mind remains our development then it can always be controlled to work towards it.

Expressing Gratitude and Appreciation:

Our internal functioning of system is so tuned that we work mechanically in a routine. We seem to have become extensions of technology and work like robots a lot of times. As the needs of life be, so do the actions of ours be. This may sometimes move you away from the feeling that we are connected to so many lives around us. We need to make conscious effort to connect to them by showing our appreciation and gratitude for all they have contributed.

Scientists are of opinion that healthy relationships need to have a basic foundation of mutual appreciation. Expression of gratitude only happens when you are feeling grateful from inside. It is this feeling and emotion which moves you to take actions towards showing the same. Gratitude is an emotion that can be expressed for the smallest of things and biggest of ventures.

There should be a feeling of appreciating the goodness of life. Life can't be consistent all the time, good and bad alternate. Yet to be able to hold faith through a lean period is a form of gratitude. Sometimes the human mind envisions that their survival is independent and can happen without others contribution. This fallacy creates a feeling of pride and vanity, which has no base. To be humble towards your existence and all you have been endowed with is a requirement for balanced functioning of human beings. Sensitivity towards your fellowmen beyond you has to be in your human nature.

With greater inner kindness we can move beyond were we are and emphasize good things to   direct our lives in the in the direction we desire for it to. We will consciously have to work towards creating a new story line for us giving us abundant opportunities of appreciation around us. The aim of meditation and mind control is to awaken the freedom of mind and benevolence of heart. It balances or emotions and promotes a relaxed mind. With a mind at ease our awareness increases. When we start acknowledging all events that happen in our life we have to admit that each one of us have gratitude inspiring events too. It is a matter of fact that mind tunes in more to the negative ones and reinforces images. If the mind is diverted to notice more of the moments of joy the rest problems will seem smaller. Expressing gratitude really changes the way we see world.

Love Is Everything:

As we explore the obstacles in the path of self-realization, we need to question and examine our basic distrust in today's times. Why does trust and love take so much of effort? This question may take us back to our early environment where we grew up and the effects it had in the way we shaped up. If we were cherished and cared for that's the energy we would send out to the universe. If we neglected and uncared for that is the feeling we would impart even in our relationships. If we were lovingly held, we will lovingly hold. They say, always smile at a child, for you will in a way create better tomorrow. Love is a universal feeling which cannot be imprisoned in just human relationships. Universal and unconditional love is supposed to hold the humanity in arms and extend beyond that to the cosmos too. This expresses the harmony of the whole universe and nothing can be excluded from this. There will be ups and downs in life, positive and negative people around; even if you try to find peace through meditation and prayers others will muddle up your clear bent of mind with their unthankful, ungrateful and unloving attitude. Make your inner self so strong that your inner peace radiates out. Do not let them to pull you into darkness but bring them to your light. That's how you can share love and its everything to cause a chain reaction.

But does this happen in our lives and those around us in the way it is supposed to happen. Why is conflict more evident and ego raising its head to push out love? Pride also adds to the existing confusion. We have to understand here that before we can have a fulfilling relationship with others we need to have one with ourselves. That relation is more important in explaining our behavior towards others. When we cherish ourselves, we think ourselves to be worthy enough of accepting the gifts of life. We are then more open to the way life turns out.

Meditation makes a difference to this relation of love. With meditation the mind settles down in a calm state. With meditation not only does our attachments weaken, our prejudices are thrown away. We see everything without any hindrance. When our attachments to those we love or are primarily connected to fall off, the mind gains the capacity to be beneficial to others beyond the close-knit circle. When mind is calm it analyses thoughts with the right perspective, even in the worst of situations. Changes in brain behavior are witnessed with practice of meditation in life. When we practice of bringing a attribute in our lives, we start investing in the thought and its manifestation. When the same attribute is thought of and felt repeatedly mind brings it to reality. So, when love and compassion become natural attributes, the enlightened being in our lives is not far away.

Our Drive Is Our Values:

A life worth living is the one based on the values which are dear to us and the passions that ignite it. Lot of us just walks through life, as if through haze, with no sense of our directions or values. The materialism of today's age consumes their time and lives and they get swept away. Not realizing that sooner or later it's your conviction, values and beliefs which define you and hold you in testing times. The swaying culture of times does not stand by you. Till the time we are driven by our values we are on track. Values not only shape our actions but also decide our behavior. The day we start compromising with them, we are in for a rude shock in life. If we work in alignment with our values, our life will be most likely one we are proud of. If we don't know what we stand for and where we want to go, we will easily lose track.

Values are words which express what is important to us. They are what we think is right and valued highly. We look up to them and want our children to grow up with. Then there is no clutter in mind and we think clearly with peace, we know from the core of our heart what the right thing to do is. Values are directly linked to our beliefs too. It tells us the way we should take in our lives, what is wrong and what is right. By having these filters close to us in life it should help us to hold the right course we need to take. Awareness about values is very crucial and right values can be cultivated only on a peaceful content mind.

With meditation becoming a practice in life it gives an intention to base your life on. Meditation redirects your senses and mind from the culture of consumerism around us. When we realign we articulate our values better. Mind focuses on more valuable things than a bigger house, nice clothes and a large bank balance and so on to real things like our family, the people at work and their families, health etc. With increased awareness mind feels more grateful. This mental state promotes simple and focused life. You start appreciating things which escaped your eyes

Are Our Values Ours?

Values hold the pillars of institution called man!! Are these values really ours? Since they represent us, it is important to access that the values we carry as ours are really ours. Sometimes it so happens that we seem to be carrying values which are reflections of others life values. It is essential to know which values drive our life and which personal values do we cherish. They decide our priorities and our behaviors in life. But as we move in life our priorities, values and even definition of success changes. We realize that when we function out of the highest placed values we seem to be having a satisfying outcome. For example, when we place time and perfection as priority in our career we seem to be gaining not only in appreciation but also as faster growth in professional ladder. The moment we move away from our values we have a natural confusion in our mind because conflicts occur in carrying out our actions. We inherit values from our society from our parent's teachers, friends, spouse and so on. We cultivate our own to what we think as good and right and what needs to be followed. Finally, we follow those values that we find are carry worthy and make sense. When we meditate we become more kind and patient. Choose being human over being right and you will be right every time.

Using or being guided by meditative moments it is better to be aware of the values we hold. When we want to find what our values are we need to ask ourselves what is important to us in life? That gives us the answer. Knowing it keeps us informed about using the same in persuasive communication we use with others. They work as filters in deciding our actions and behaviors. They not only guide our ventures but also create our reality. So being grounded to them keeps us close to our desired goal.

Thoughts, Its Inherent Energy and Manifestation

Our brain has been bestowed with the job of thinking, which it does without any interruption. The mind is so good at jumping from one thought to another in fraction of moments. It goes from one association to another set-in seconds, clear thinking gets lost in this these transactions of thoughts. Once we are able to control this continuous chatter, our thoughts are less scattered and more directed and focused. Thoughts are our own energy manifested into our reality. To an untrained mind it becomes difficult to focus our thoughts the way we want. But meditation helps in channelizing our thoughts, in the direction we want.

Meditation works towards getting mastery on how thought process works. Brain keeps sending thoughts, it now depends on us to encourage or discourage the ones we want to interpret. Mind has a habit of sending a trailer before the actual thought. For example, "why didn't he message me throughout the day? Is he seeing someone else? "Now this may lead to the complete train of thoughts regarding the same. If we encourage the first link, it will produce the chain or break the link if discouraged. The thoughts pass on in a second if not recognized immediately. Meditation allows us to slow down these thoughts and increase the time between each. Once the mind gets into disciplining process it is able to concentrate more and fall less to distractions around.

Descartes, father of modern philosophy rightly pointed to both, the defining trait and also the curse on all human beings by his statement,

"I think. Therefore, I am".

So it means, the person is all about his thoughts. We need to watch our thoughts, observe them. There is no need to judge them, yet to notice and observe will go a long way. Let the mind be given only truth and be fed with the right thoughts. Purer the mind, it is easier to control. The more just a person, the lesser he has to worry about and the lesser chaos in mind. Once we are systematically able to tame our mind it is endowed with calmness. We become one with our own consciousness and life occurrences become easier to follow.

Tap In The Inner You:

We have always been reflective about our sense of being, our consciousness and who we are? As we understand more about the way our brain works and reacts to various stimuli, these questions slowly stand answered in bits and pieces. When we undertake meditation, we are more in sync with our own mind and consciousness as well with the universe at large. With meditation we are able to tap our inner resources and realize that the potential to grow is granted to all human beings. Sometimes we are unable to locate it and sometimes we overlook it since the talent comes to us without any effort. We undermine its value. Let's begin to acknowledge what is within us and start respecting and valuing it. When we do that we become engaged with our inner self and its energy. Let us work towards our true calling and tap the inner reservoir, to move with unwavering desire and passion to achieve. Believe again to achieve!

Conclusion:

The journey of life sometimes teaches you lessons, in a way, you never expected it to, and yet you end up learning. That is the way of life. My journey continues on a positive note as I decided to go through challenges and remove severe health issue and continue to create a niche for myself and others. The ground of fearlessness is fear. In order to become fearless, you have to stand in the middle of your fear and face it. It is then that you can rise out of it. As a human "I am" is what I should want to be, not what my circumstances around want me to be. My identity transforms due to my intent and efforts, the power to be, is lying muted within. Unleash it and let the universe send out positivity to make you reach your optimum potential. Harvest the power of thought in your favor and learn to use the unlimited supply of thought "seeds" to reinvent your belief system if at all it begins to limit your growth. If it has been a challenging life for you till now, decide to let it change henceforth. The clutches of your own "ego" may want to pull you and your growth as a successful individual down, accept the reach of its clutches and get over the "I am better" attitude and let your learning happen.

The vicious cycles of mind are always at play. The thoughts in it come out either dipped in positivity or limiting negativity; the choice is fortunately in your hands. Decide the color of your thoughts, being fully aware and conscious about it. The seeds of doubt get in before you can even think about them, let them not seep in and poison the mind. Their roots spread much faster than imaginable to mind, to actually overshadow the real you in your own mind. Let pure thoughts take birth to attract the same purity and positivity from the universe to push your wheels of success. Hold still to your faith as this happens and invest in your actions towards others. Your karma ultimately decides your luck. Sow well to reap well..., can it be any other way? Destiny will then seem to be as you desire it to be. There has always been ultimate justice at cosmic level and that cannot ever go wrong.

Learn to believe in your own self even when no one believes in you. Keep feeding your faith, the doubts of any kind will perish into their own deserving death. In spite of this there come moments when some hidden unfounded fears poke their heads out to draw disharmony into human lives. They then need to be dealt with then and there, silencing them forever by actually dealing with them. A peaceful mind raised on prayers to the universe and humankind will always find it easier to do it than minds still chasing unwanted fears. Gratitude filled heart and love for mankind make your journey as human being easier to do.

Life challenges are not sent into our lives to paralyze us, rather we soon discover, they are supposed to help us discover who we are!! Keeping a positive attitude gives us the power over our circumstances, rather than the other way around, so keeping our chin up will only help. As we overcome our life situations, sharing the outcome will help assess our own growth besides stimulating others. This then gives us the inspiration to take challenges in other aspects of our lives. Keep a diary to track the way we make progress, depending on that the targets in future can be set. Just wanting something in life will not bring about the changes you have been working for, you have to aspire for it in all desperation. The hunger from within should be so compelling that the obstacles become irrelevant in the process.

Certain life skills become very effective in making your resolve towards life changing decisions to happen. Life skills have been enabling individuals to not just have satisfying lives themselves but also helping others as enablers. Tools in today's times like NLP, Hypnotherapy and counseling have the ability to enhance the existing ones in an individual. It hence becomes important to access these important tools to aid the functioning our lives. Working on communication and language skills enables effective communication channels and better understanding leading to fundamental rapport building in different spheres of life. Handling a state of mind and channelizing it towards a positive mode helps beyond expectations. Be always on the lookout for pushing your own self outside your comfort zone, the biggest challenge is to not be content in boundaries of our comfort zone and putting onus on fate. Consider the rewards of going into unknown waters and coming out victorious. Let that stay as your motivation. We all deal with fear, uncertainty and seeds of self-doubt, yet to keep these feelings away from dictating your actions remain the biggest challenge. Inner demons have a habit of resurfacing at intervals and to keep a watch is important. To seek a mentor or enabler or a counselor in today's times is much easier than ever before and hence the path of self-development and personal growth has less obstacles.

The truth of life is change, yet the most important part of life is accepting the fact and moving ahead. Somewhere in life certain decisions need to be taken and the risk of them turning out whichever way needs to be completely understood. Trusting yourself at such moments is important. Failure or success have never been destinations, they have been stops in a journey so none of them can be the end!! Moving forward is all that counts and the attitude & intent matters more than what is encountered at end. A caring and honest support system behind you, journaling your journey and keeping up your efforts at all costs is what matters. Imagine the day when u can finally say "I did it" ! When you can say I never gave up and I did not quit. When these moments of trials become memories for that goal you reached, you will thank yourself for the rest of your life. Transformations happen and they happen soon if you persist hard enough. Always remember why you began in the first place, let that be your motivation on your path and soon you will reach were you always wanted to be. Just care enough for you to begin the journey in the first! Life is less of what happens to you and more of how you respond to it!!! Nurture the gift of life and move on.

www.ingramcontent.com/pod-product-compliance
Lightning Source LLC
Chambersburg PA
CBHW051056250726
48656CB00001B/320